ON AIR

Insider Secrets to Attract the Media and Get Free Publicity

ON AIR
Insider Secrets to Attract the Media and Get Free Publicity

BROADCAST YOUR BUSINESS WITH

KATRINA CRAVY
EMMY AWARD-WINNING REPORTER AND TV HOST

HenschelHAUS Publishing, Inc.
Milwaukee, Wisconsin

Copyright © 2016 by Katrina Cravy, Inc.
All rights reserved.

This book is copyrighted. No part of this book or eBook may be reproduced or transmitted in any form or by any means, electronic or mechanical, including photocopying, recording or by any information storage and retrieval system, without written permission from the author.

Images used with permission.

BOOK DISCLAIMER
By using this book, you accept this disclaimer in full. Nothing in Katrina Cravy, Inc.'s materials or its website is a promise or guarantee of obtaining free advertising via television or any other media means; neither is it any promise or guarantee of any growth of your business or business earnings.

There are no representations or warranties, express or implied, about the completeness, accuracy, reliability, suitability, or availability with respect to the information, products, services, or related graphics contained in this book for any purpose. Neither author or publisher assumes and hereby disclaims any liability to any party for any loss, damage, or disruption caused by errors or omissions, whether such errors or omissions result from accident, negligence, or any other cause.

Links from Katrina Cravy, Inc.'s Site to other sites do not constitute an endorsement from Katrina Cravy, Inc. These links are provided for information only. As a purchaser, it is your responsibility to determine the content and usefulness of information you find on other sites.

Published by
HenschelHAUS Publishing, Inc.
www.henschelHAUSbooks.com

ISBN: 978159598-505-7
E-ISBN: 978159598-506-4
Audio ISBN: 978159598-507-1
LCCN: 2016954364

Publisher's Cataloging-In-Publication Data
(Prepared by The Donohue Group, Inc.)
Names: Cravy, Katrina.
Title: On air : insider secrets to attract the media and get free publicity : broadcast your
    business / with Katrina Cravy, Emmy Award-winning reporter and TV host.
Description: Milwaukee, Wisconsin : HenschelHAUS Publishing, Inc., [2016]
Identifiers: LCCN 2016954364 | ISBN 978-1-59598-505-7 | ISBN
    978-1-59598-506-4 (ebook) | ISBN 978-1-59598-507-1 (audiobook)
Subjects: LCSH: Industrial publicity. | Television in publicity. | Selling. | Business
    communication. | Mass media and business.
Classification: LCC HD59 .C73 2016 (print) | LCC HD59 (ebook) | DDC 659.2--dc23

Cover design by Dan Fleming

Printed in the United States of America

*This book is dedicated to Mom and Dad.
They told me I could do anything I want, as long as I
worked hard and treated people right.
I hope you got the same message.*

*The co-dedication (is there such a thing?) goes to my
awesome husband, Scott, and my wonderful son, Billy.
They are my life.*

*This guide is for all the entrepreneurs,
experts, and super-smart people I've met over the years
who take the leap to lead.
Your passion for what you do is electrifying
and I want to be near you.
Let's broadcast your message and energy to everyone.*

TABLE OF CONTENTS

This Book is for You! 1
Preface (or "So Here's How All This Happened") 5

Chapter 1: The "Magic Box" 17
Chapter 2: Do You H.A.V.E. What It Takes? 25
Chapter 3: Being Booked As An Expert 51
Chapter 4: How To Write A Killer Email 97
Chapter 5: Making The Perfect Phone Pitch 109
Chapter 6: Hey, This is a LIVE Report
    From Your Business! 117
Chapter 7: You Survived TV!
    Guess What Happens Now?! 125
Chapter 8: Yes, YOU Can Hold A Press Conference 145
Chapter 9: Free Stuff, Local Celebrity Status,
    and Clever Ideas 157
Final Thoughts 175

Acknowledgments 179
About the Author / Broadcast Your Business 183

This book is for you!

Thank you so much for buying this book! Please thank the friend or search engine that said, "You have to read this!"

I hope I get to meet you in person someday. I know the world is waiting to fall in love with your story. I can't wait to listen and help you tell it to a huge audience. Until then, here's my introduction.

I wrote this book because people always ask me, "Hey, Katrina, how do I get on your show?"

Honestly, it's not *MY* show. However, after more than 20 years of being "on" in people's homes, we have a relationship.

I love talking to people and I appreciate the trust they have in me to provide real answers. Many know me as a problem-solving consumer reporter who cuts through the red tape.

Now I want to cut through the mystery of getting booked on television and outline what you need to do to broadcast YOUR business—***ON AIR***.

If you've ever wondered, "How did that person get booked on that show? Why did that company get the feature story?" I'm the person to ask.

As an Emmy Award-winning consumer reporter, anchor, and talk-show host, I've set up thousands of interviews and booked hundreds of guests.

Just like anything in life, you can follow all the instructions and you won't get what you want all the time. For whatever reason, the stars might not align and you won't grab the media's attention on the first pass.

Don't worry. Keep trying and feel free to contact me by email at Katrina.Cravy@KatrinaCravy.com or on Facebook, Twitter, or LinkedIn for additional coaching and ideas.

The communication and marketing skills you're about to learn will also help you communicate better in life. *Extra bonus.*

I know what the media really wants and I've come up with an easy formula to see if you H.A.V.E. what it takes.

You're about to learn how to craft a killer email with the perfect pitch and produce a TV segment that will make TV producers call you—ultimately bringing customers straight to your business or organization.

If you don't have a big marketing budget and are looking for some publicity, there are some tricks to get you the coverage you need for *FREE!*

This Book is for You!

If you're a:
- Business ready to highlight a product/service
- Person who dreams of being the go-to expert in your field
- Charity or organization with an awesome event
- Public Relations Specialist who wants the title of "Rock Star"

Don't be shy! Step up and say, "HEY, Katrina, point the spotlight on us!! Get us on air! Help us broadcast our business."

Again, thanks for your trust. I promise this journey will be fun—and worth it!

—Katrina Cravy

PREFACE
(OR "SO HERE'S HOW THIS ALL HAPPENED")

I always wanted to be an entrepreneur. Something about grabbing the bull by the horns and going for a risky ride is amazing to me. Business owners are bold!

Luckily, my job allowed me to meet thousands of people like you until I was ready to make the leap myself.

Every person has such an amazing story. I've been blessed to be able to help people tell their stories in a way viewers will remember.

I've also been asked countless times to tell *my* story and reveal what life is really like behind the scenes of a television station. I say "countless" because after 20 years, I didn't write down all the times I've emceed an event, given keynote speeches to big audiences, or stopped by for a quick Rotary meeting talk. (If you're into accurate numbers, like my husband, I'm sure the number of appearances could be counted. I just don't want to take the time.)

This book, my consulting, speaking, and actually my whole company, were inspired when I was asked to give a speech to a women's entrepreneur group in March 2013.

For some reason, I didn't feel like doing the standard "How I Got into Journalism" talk and going through the typical Q & A session. You know, the "Do you do your own hair and makeup?" questions. (Yes, I do.)

I told my husband, "I really want to give these women something they can use." I'd fallen out of love with my life story and I knew I needed to make my message about THEM.

Announcing the Women's Journey event on Real Milwaukee in 2013.
(Photo courtesy of FOX 6 News, Milwaukee)

Golden Rule: Know Your Audience

I personally think this rule should immediately follow, "Treat others like you want to be treated."

After two weeks of tinkering and typing, I was praying for direction. My husband came home and said, "My mom wanted me to give you the heads-up that her friend's son started a business and he wants to know what to do to get on TV." That sealed the deal. I would completely answer the question people always ask me, "How do I get on TV?"

I gave the speech and the response was OVERWHELMING!! Out of nearly 180 women, about thirty stood in line afterwards to tell me about their businesses and get my suggestions for how to market to the media.

They realized that getting on air, appearing on TV for a few minutes, was worth thousands of dollars.

Companies pay that much or more for one 30-second commercial. Imagine what 3 or 4 minutes during an actual broadcast is worth!

You'll be presenting yourself in front of thousands of people, which can only boost your brand and boost your sales. Not to mention, you can take the segment and blast your awesome performance all over social media for more sales.

The best part? The media needs great local stories and compelling content, which is a win-win combo for everyone.

Here's a chunk from my speech that night:

> Good evening, what a special night to be surrounded by so many beautiful and amazing women here to meet and support each other.
>
> I'm honored Ami asked me to speak tonight because I think what she is doing with this group is extraordinary and quite frankly, the invitation gave me a deadline to say something meaningful.
>
> You would think speaking would be easy for me. I talk to hundreds of thousands of people every day on TV either with my consumer reports for Contact 6 or hot topics on Real Milwaukee or Studio A. But saying something meaningful to a group of business women is a different story.
>
> Let me start by telling you—I am in awe of you. My mother had her own real estate company with one of her closest friends when I was growing up. I saw the triumphs and the trials they went through. Just the fact you're an entrepreneur trying to make something happen makes you a winner to me.
>
> Few people have the guts you have to strike out on their own, and that makes me want to get to know you better.
>
> I'm going to share some of my experiences and then open the talk up for questions at the end, so I can find out what you really need to make your business succeed.

PREFACE

I got my start in journalism in 8th grade at Clark Intermediate School in Clovis, California. I was a writer for the Xeroxed paper handed out to my classmates. Pretty big deal.

My assignment was to write about the Title IX requirement "separate but equal," which was enacted to give girls the same opportunities as boys. My teacher asked me to focus on one question. She wanted me to ask the principal, "Why were the boys the only ones who were allowed to use the real gym for basketball?"

The girls had to practice at Veterans Memorial Building across the street. The floor there was cracked and bowed so much you literally had to hit the pot holes just right to pass the ball to your teammate.

The crazy thing was the girls practiced at Veterans Memorial every day and then played their games in the nice gym on campus. The team never really had home court advantage.

I asked the principal lots of questions and I liked getting to talk to an adult like an adult. As my final follow-up question, I asked, "If you had to make a decision today, who would you give the gym too?" He thought for half a beat and said, "The boys."

I said, "Okay, thank you very much," and left. I really didn't care at the time because I didn't play basketball, plus I was 12, and I wasn't going to argue with the principal.

I wrote the article and then something big happened. My article was censored. The principal refused to Xerox my story! (Insert gasp.) But my teacher wasn't happy, and she made her feelings known.

The athletic director was yelling at me. The boys weren't happy, and basically I could say goodbye to a basketball player ever asking me out. The decision about the article went all the way up to the Superintendent's office!

My friends thought I was in big trouble. (Kids love this part of the story.) My parents showed up at the school to meet with the principal and defend me. I really didn't know what was going on. I just knew I was causing a stir, and I liked it!!

Plus, guess what? Ultimately the administration reconsidered its decision and the principal changed his mind.

After my article, the real gym and practice time at Veterans Memorial was split evenly between the boys and the girls.

By the time I went to high school journalism class, the teacher said, "Oh, I've heard of you."

Eleven years later, when I was already working across country at a TV station, I came home for a visit. My dad and I just happened to be driving past Clark Intermediate after school and saw the boys dribbling the balls over to the Veterans Memorial building for practice.

He punched me in the arm and smiled.

Those kids had no idea another kid changed the rules so long ago.

The experience was exhilarating because I made a difference and adults were listening to me. I saw power in journalism and I didn't let it go.

After graduating from the University of Southern California with a degree in Broadcast Journalism and

Preface

Political Science, I landed my first TV job in Parkersburg, West Virginia. Does anybody know where that is?

New York City is market #1. Chicago is market #5. Parkersburg, West Virginia was market #195.

With everything I owned packed into boxes or into my Toyota Corolla, I drove across country for a job that paid less than local fast food places.

With my $100,000 education, I took a job for $15,000. My grandfather begged me to come back and manage Taco Bell.

Success takes sacrifice.

I was paid six dollars an hour. Most people think overtime is paid at time and a half. However, when we went into overtime we were paid half-time—so three bucks an hour.

On Saturday and Sunday evenings, I always worked overtime to anchor the nightly news at 11 o'clock. Technically to anchor a half-hour show, I was paid a $1.50.

I always figured if anybody ever called to complain, I'd say," Hey, you got what you paid for," and then I'd hang up.

I was in Parkersburg, West Virginia, for about six months before I started sending out my resume tape hoping that another, bigger station, would pick me up. You know I was 23 and on my way to the TODAY show.

I had sent out about 40 tapes and been rejected by the 80- and 60-size markets before I received a call from Channel 4's News Director in Milwaukee. Are you kidding me? That's market 35! He hired me during the interview.

Success can be a surprise.

I was a general assignment reporter and the job was awesome. I had moved up the chain enough that when the Packers won the NFC conference game, the boss called and put me on a plane to New Orleans the next day to start our Super Bowl coverage.

For two weeks, I highlighted the Big Easy. One of the highlights for me was tracking down Brett Favre's parents and being invited to their house in Kiln to talk about their Super Bowl son. The amazing interview came complete with video of them pulling toilet paper out of their trees. Their neighbors thought teepeeing their house was an appropriate gift for getting into the Super Bowl.

(Left) First stop was Brett Favre's hometown, Kiln, Mississippi.
(Right) The view broadcasting "live" above Bourbon Street in New Orleans.
(January, 1997).

The Packers won and all was right with the world, except not for long. Shortly after, I was cut.

Without warning and close to the end of my contract, I was called in and told, "You're not our first choice to go, but you are the first contract that's coming up and we need the money from your reporter position to make a producer position."

Basically, we won't need your services any more. I wasn't fired. I was non-renewed. Whatever you call it, I was devastated.

I also had a non-compete clause in my contract stating I could not work for any other station in the local market for one year, even though two stations were interested.

Success takes setbacks.

I was on unemployment. I tried to keep my spirits up by sending out resume tapes in the morning and playing golf in the afternoon. I didn't get to play for long because two months later, a station in Portland, Oregon called. That's in the 20 market range. Now we're talking.

Something bigger, plus part-time anchoring too, so something better. God has a way.

If one person doesn't think you are worth it, someone else will. The trick is finding that person and no matter what others say, knowing your own worth.

I loved Portland and was grateful to see the city from above as the helicopter reporter. Flying was a blast. But I only spent one year there and then I felt drawn back to my friends and the people I love in Milwaukee.

Channel 6 hired me as a general assignment reporter. After six months, I was called into the office and told that

Tom Hopper would be retiring and they thought I would be the right person to take over Contact 6. For those of you who aren't from Milwaukee, Tom Hopper was a BIG deal. Since 1972, he ran Contact 6, a consumer problem-solving unit. If you have a consumer problem, Contact 6 goes to bat for you and cuts through the red tape. Our ultimate goal is to work out a resolution with the company or organization you have an issue with and get your money back.

I thought they were crazy at first. Stepping into those shoes was unimaginable. I said I would go home and think about it. Pray about it.

I really didn't want the job, and then I started thinking about my time at Clark Intermediate and the change I made there. This was an opportunity to make a difference in people's lives. I knew I was called to take this opportunity.

Success takes starting.

Sometimes you just have to say yes.

For some reason, I said "yes" when Ami asked me to speak to you tonight.

Usually I would say "no." This is my family time and a non-station event. I'm not getting paid to do this, so why did I?

First, Ami approached me with a smile. Her body language and soul told me that she really cared, and therefore I should. Also this group intrigued me: women in business, women entrepreneurs, women trying to get a fresh start, and make something happen. Lord, what could I say to these women?

I said to myself, "Delilah (because that's what I like to call myself, [*laugh*]), figure out what makes you tick and see if it's worthy to share with them." Then the idea hit me!

I have knowledge I forget I have because I've been doing this for 20 years.

I know how we end up booking people on our shows, or getting a reporter and photographer to come to your business.

As business women, you need exposure. I'm not talking Kim Kardashian exposure, but real publicity. Get people talking about your product, your business, and really YOU.

Once, when I was doing a story about an historical building, a news director told me, "People don't care about things; they care about people." So true.

We have to make the audience care about YOU before we make them care enough to buy what you're selling.

And this is how we're going to do it..."

Several months later, I took the brief information in my 30-minute talk, listened to the questions people were asking, and started writing this book.

Chapter 1

THE "MAGIC BOX"

You know you want success. You want your company, your organization, or your personal reputation to take off and soar. Your product and/or your knowledge are great, and could really make a difference in people's lives—if only more people knew about it.

So what's the key to getting on TV? My promise to you is, by the time you finish this book, you'll know how to master the "Magic Box" and the people who hold it.

Why do I call it a "Magic Box"? Funny you should ask.

When I worked in West Virginia, our sports anchor came out of a store and a little girl spotted him in the parking lot. She grabbed her father's leg and said, "Daddy, Daddy, there's the man in the magic box."

We all laughed about what she said when he told us and I realized two things. First, parents really should explain things better to their children, and secondly, TV truly can be a "MAGIC BOX."

To me, life is strange because when we see people in person, they don't seem all that important. However, when we limit our field of vision and shrink them down into the "Magic Box," suddenly they seem special. People look up to a so-called expert or a person pushing a product—simply because that person is on TV.

If the same person simply knocked on your front door to get the sale, rather than appearing on TV, you'd be skeptical. You might not even open the door. However, if that same person is on air, he or she is instantly invited in, perhaps into every room in the house, and greeted with immediate credibility.

How would you like that type of greeting?

Viewers trust that the news station has done its homework and chosen these people for a good reason.

For the most part, yes, we have done our homework. However, the truth is show producers and reporters are really looking for people who make good TV too. We need to "hold" our viewers and keep their fingers away from the dreaded channel changer.

If you are a start-up company or new organization, we'll check out your website and some of the credentials you claim to have, but honestly, we are going with our guts and will decide whether the segment pitch idea is good.

For example, a local cleaning company or money-saving blogger wants to show our viewers how to make cheaper cleaning supplies by simply using lemons or products people already have at home. *Sold!*

I'll tell you why in a minute.

Pantry items to the rescue for household cleaning problems.
(Photo courtesy of FOX 6 News, Milwaukee)

Once the station double-checks to see if you really are a member of the Better Business Bureau or Chamber of Commerce like you claim, then you have the job.

Becoming an "Expert"

Maybe you don't have a product to sell at all. Maybe you are a person with lots of initials after your name or an author with supreme knowledge about a certain subject. We need you too.

We need to know you have experience, as well as an awesome resume. Remember, Google is only a step away. Just like other folks, we are going to check out your website and social media accounts.

Does Your Headshot Picture Look Professional or Are You Doing a Keg Stand?

I know you're thinking "that's obvious," but you'd be surprised how often we research someone online only to find party pictures and images that don't show them in the best light.

Your professional life is different from your personal life; don't mix the two on social media. A wise choice would be keeping professional Facebook and Twitter pages, and then another one for your friends and family.

When you send us the email with your credentials and all your links, you can direct us to the "professional" side of you.

Key point: *Invest in a professional headshot! A picture taken by your friend just doesn't have the right look.*

Does the Content You Provide Seem Knowledgeable and Easy to Understand?

If the information you wish to share is too complex, then it won't work. Brain surgery might seem simple to you, but what if you were explaining the procedure and the benefits to my ten-year-old son?

Take out all the industry jargon and break down your methods, or how your product works, into "layman's terms." This task often isn't easy and that's when coaching helps.

Check out the language on your website too. After you send out a press release, or email pitch an idea, the media usually goes to your website first. If the information there is too difficult to understand, or the overall look of the page is confusing, we'll assume you can't break it down when you're on the air either.

Make your message easy for us and for our viewers to understand. And because you claim to be an expert, we're going to dig a little deeper.

Producers like to know you are already a leader recognized by a business organization, a local college, or a local hospital. Basically, another organization has already signed off on you.

If the main hospital in town says you're the number-one doctor to detect and treat pathological

---

"Magic Box" Job Descriptions

Executive Producer: Manages the producers, host, reporters, photojournalists, and the overall direction of the show.

Producer: Manages the show, chooses the content, the amount of time a segment or story receives, and where it runs in the order of the show.

Director: Is responsible for the look of the show, where the guest and host will sit, what camera shots to take, plus manages the crew.

lying, we'll interview you. Then if someone reveals you lied about where you went to college, well…the hospital is going to take the bigger public relations hit, not us.

Develop affiliations with associations or groups to increase your credibility, and don't lie on your resume!

Questions to ask yourself:

- Whatcha got for the "Magic Box"?
- What's your area of expertise?
- What product or service do you want to show off?

How Much Do You Know About Your Local Programs?

You've been working so hard lately you probably haven't had a lot of time to watch news programs, but it's time. You need to see what's "selling," especially on the morning shows.

In most television markets across the country, the morning shows have to fill 2 to 5 hours of time. That's where you come in.

Morning shows give you the best chance of getting some air time. If you want to share your knowledge and expertise, watch how others are presenting themselves.

Personally, I believe many are doing it wrong.

They're doing sit-down interviews with the host and they're dry and boring. I don't think any viewer

The "Magic Box"

walks away remembering anything at all about the segment.

I want to help you do it right. I want to help you super-charge the segment and have the producers begging you to come back again. You're going to break through with your enthusiasm and your ability to "produce" your own segment.

Think of producing as the way you use the time you're on the "Magic Box." Just like any magic trick, you need to know the answers to some trade secrets.

For example:

- What goes into the perfect story or segment so you can make the right pitch?
- How should you write a "killer email" to get a reporter or producer's attention?
- What is the best time to send that email or make that call?
- How do you know you're contacting the right person for your subject?
- What should you wear when you get booked?
- How should your display table look?
- What sound bites should you put into your conversation?
- What's the best way to interact with the host or reporter before and after you've met them?

- How do you get the station to link to your website?
- How long does the station usually keep your segment on its website?
- How should you record the story or segment so you can use it on your website and through social media later?
- What can you give of value to anchors/reporters to share through their social media channels? Even if they don't book you?
- After you've been on once, when can you pitch the station again?
- Should you pitch all local stations with your story, or be loyal to one?
- How do you get the story on the network's national feed to send to other local affiliates?
- What creative ideas can you come up with to land on local TV?

This book will answer all those questions and more. After reading it, if you think you need some one-on-one coaching to create the segment and boost your performance, I'm just a click away at KatrinaCravy.com.

Chapter 2
DO YOU H.A.V.E. WHAT IT TAKES?

After more than 20 years of booking experts for my stories or guests for the shows I've been on, I know what the media wants from people. I know the trade secrets.

Honestly, though, getting free publicity isn't a real secret. No one is keeping the "television" code locked up in a vault or hidden at the tippy-tippy top of a TV tower.

Television is like any other business. You don't really understand what "they" do, and how "they" do it, unless you're on the inside.

After giving my first speech to "A Woman's Journey" business owners, I knew from their kind comments I was taking them "inside" and unlocking useful information. After hearing all this love, how could anybody not want to pour out her heart and mind and share what she knows?

I knew I wanted to speak to business groups all over the country. Not long after my presentation, I sat down and started writing this book. I also called the Wisconsin Women's Business Initiative Corporation (WWBIC) to see if they'd like me to volunteer and teach a real class to their clients. They said, "YES!"

For WWBIC, I spent hours coming up with the curriculum, making a work sheet, and learning how to do a PowerPoint presentation. Yikes…no director in the control room. Scary.

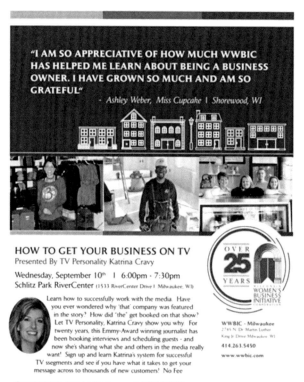

WWBIC flyer announcing the event

I also figured out a real system to see if you H.A.V.E. what it takes to get a spot on TV. As part of the class, I also created break-out, small-group sessions for people to help each other make their publicity pitch that night.

Pretty quickly, I discovered that I loved teaching. The response from the people taking the course was great. It is still part of the day-training I do for organizations and public relation firms who want to develop their employees into media machines.

Being successful on air is all about looking at what makes a great TV story or segment, and then providing all the elements.

"Insider Secrets to Shine on Local TV" was a hit with WWBIC.

There are four essential ingredients you must H.A.V.E. to create a *Segment that Sells* for TV producers —and for you and your business.

KATRINA'S H.A.V.E. FORMULA

- **H**—"Hook." Give the media a reason why you should be on the show NOW.
- **A**—Audience Benefit. How will the viewer benefit from your message?
- **V**—Visual. Do you have a great video/product demonstration/props, and so on.
- **E**— Engaging Interview. You as the presenter or expert bring energy to the screen.

Seems simple, but rarely are we pitched an idea that meets everything we like to H.A.V.E. for a segment or story.

If you're starting to panic right now thinking of the camera and all those eyeballs on you, take a deep breath. I have some ways to build your confidence and keep you focused on the end game—reaching new customers.

Imagine how good you're going to feel when you nail the interview. Champagne for everyone!

Really, I'm serious. We're going to have champagne. Having a bit of bubbly is customary when you go through a life-altering event. You're going to be going into the world with more confidence, more poise, and a feeling of pride in your accomplishments.

Let's dive deeper.

The "Hook"

Luring in viewers takes special bait. If you're smart, you will be an attractive and timely media morsel.

To be timely, you need to know what's happening in the news or society right NOW, and have something worthwhile to say—or better yet, SHOW.

THE NOW BAIT

The NOW bait works best on TV producers who need to fill a segment on the current news. You have to pitch them your idea right away. Once the hot topic has passed, the opportunity has too.

If gas prices are shooting sky high, and you are a mechanic or own an auto dealership, can you explain why and give some tips to make sure our cars are conserving gas and saving money?

Can you:

- Bring an air compressor and a tire into the studio?
- Show the host and viewers how to read the code on the tire and where to find the right tire pressure?
- Show us how to properly inflate the tire?
- Tell us how much we can save over the year with this information.

- Better yet, how about some goggles for the host to wear and see if they can fill the tire correctly?

The compressor will be loud and that's GREAT for a short burst. Nothing like an odd, loud noise on TV to make sure the viewer comes to the screen to see what's happening.

What you *say* should benefit the audience, while at the same time, benefit you and your company. Having your face and name on the screen builds credibility. Start thinking.

Do you have something to say about what is currently happening in your hometown, your state, or even the nation? We need local experts on local and national topics, and you need customers to know you're available to provide solutions.

Be timely and better yet, be timely and create something NEW!

The NEW Bait

Everyone loves something new. It's human nature. Once we've had something for a while, even if the product or experience is still great, we get bored and are ready to move on.

If you have a product or service that's NEW, you had better start shouting it from the mountain tops, or in this case—a TV station. Especially if the NEW product solves a major problem or household dilemma.

Like Mr. Lid—

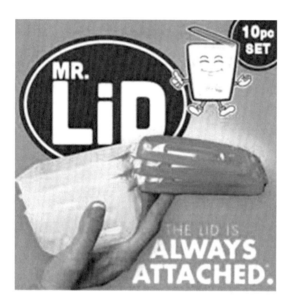

Can you believe this product? The whole premise of the company's infomercial is "no more searching for the right lid." A possible solution to a problem we all have experienced.

If I hear my husband grunting or taking a huge "this drives me crazy" breath one more time, I'll go crazy myself. I'm not sure why I feel personally responsible for our plastics problem, because I'm not the only one who puts stuff away, but Mr. Lid has shut this down tight.

Mr. Lid should really be called *Mrs.* Lid. I was told the wife of a plastics maker in Sussex, Wisconsin, really came up with the idea after putting away the leftovers from Thanksgiving. She was frustrated and turned to her husband to say something like, "You own a plastics company. Figure out a way to attach the lids so we're not always looking for them."

Keith Everson listened to his wife and Mr. Lid has been a huge success for his plastics company, Sussex IM, and for Norman Direct, another Wisconsin company that markets, packages, and sells products with the "AS SEEN ON TV" strategy. When my TV story aired in 2016, they had already sold 30 million boxes of Mr. Lids!

With both companies being local, choosing to highlight them was a no-brainer.

The product was NEW, it solved plastic container problems for our viewers, plus if our viewers had their own brilliant ideas, I showed them how to submit their idea to Norman Direct.

TV stations are always looking for something new to benefit the viewer—especially around the holidays.

The Holiday "Hook"

"Coming up, how to find new and unique gifts for Christmas, Mother's Day, Father's Day, Valentine's Day…right after the break."

How many times have we seen TV host say these words?

People want to shop from the comfort of their homes and your product needs to be featured on a display table in this gift segment.

How to you do get what you're selling up front and center? Try to think like TV producers. We're always trying to come up with fun segments for the viewers around all of these social events.

Take Christmas, for example. I happened to be writing this section of the book two weeks before Christmas and on our talk show one afternoon, we mixed cocktails made with herring. Yes, drinks with chucks of fish floating in them.

How in the world did a herring-packing company get us to go for this pitch? The concoction sounds disgusting and luckily, my boss wouldn't allow me to drink alcoholic beverages on air.

Ma Baensch Herring made an appearance on TV because the company is LOCAL. When you have a show highlighting the places and people of Milwaukee, being local is a huge selling point.

Pickled Herring Cocktail for your New Year's celebration.
(Photo courtesy of FOX 6 News, Milwaukee)

The fish-packing place also gave us something we desperately needed—a fresh, NEW idea. We also added the extra bait (*See what I did there?*) of making the segment interactive and visual. Kim Wall, the owner, brought the ingredients, dressed up our display table, and taught us how to mix the drink on live TV.

The crazy thing is that the segment almost didn't make the cut because of a near-crucial mistake on the pitch idea email. (I'll explain what was so wrong and what you should do in Chapter 4—*How to Write a Killer Email Pitch.*)

Think about what you're selling. Could your perfume company's products work on a Mother's Day segment on the most popular fragrances?

Could your spice shop work for a seasonal story? For example, the right fresh herbs to create a super spring salad, or the perfect spice to spice up your hot chocolate this winter.

Because most TV stations gear shows primarily to women, what kind of "hook" can you find for them or their kids? Typically, local television stations target women between the ages of 25 and 54. We, like our advertisers, know this is the group holding the purse strings and making the money decisions.

I'm sure you can think of the right "Hook," but if you're having trouble, call me for some one-on-one coaching. I pride myself on being able to create the right bait—and I like to fish!

How to Find the "Hook" for a Service

As a problem-solving consumer reporter, I once did a story at a great inner-city daycare and elementary facility which had unfortunately been ripped off by a fundraising scam.

While the photographer was shooting "B-roll" (extra video), I started talking with Executive Director Tamara Johnson. She told me Malaika Early Learning Center had been honored for its work, but only received news coverage when a stray bullet from a drive-by shooting ripped through the wall.

Thankfully no one was hurt, but I felt badly because I know the media focuses on the negative.

Tamara's facility was beautiful and the kids were smart and well-behaved. She explained she had a terrific board of directors, support from local charities, and still, she felt no one in the community knew the school was there.

Lucky for her, I'd just given my "Pushing for Publicity" speech and my wheels were churning out advice.

Spring break was right around the corner and parents needed cool projects to keep their kids busy. I figured Tamara had plenty of activities to share.

Tamara's area of expertise was 3- to 5-year-olds. I asked her if she, or an instructor plus three kids, could come to the station and do a craft demonstration.

She immediately said yes. From there, we began to construct how she should produce her time on the "Magic Box" and achieve what a great TV segment needs to H.A.V.E.

At the time, I hadn't thought through this formula. Now I know it works.

I asked if she could bring children who were ethnically diverse, since TV stations need to reach a broad audience. We are all simply attracted to people who look like us. TV producers need to cast a wide net that mirrors the entire community and encourages more viewers to watch.

A fun project idea for your kids.
(Photo courtesy of FOX 6 News, Milwaukee)

To make the segment even cuter, I asked if she could bring in a small table with chairs where the kids could do their project.

Tamara took all my ideas and not only did the segment look great, the craft time was useful for parents and fun to watch.

We then placed a link to the instructions for the art project on the station's website, which gave her additional publicity. The host mentioned the name of the Center in the introductions and Malaika Early Learning Center was put up on the screen under the teachers' names, plus Tamara got the additional website hit. All for FREE!

A is for Audience Benefit

Think about the viewers. Now consider how your product, service, or message is going to benefit them. What can you "promise" them?

Remember the example of the local cleaning company promising to show you how to make inexpensive cleaners with products you already have in your home? That cleaning company would get the gig, because its lesson would benefit our viewers by saving them money.

"Segments that Sell" to producers H.A.V.E. great benefits/promises for the viewers.

Most common benefits or promises:

- Saves them money
- Saves them time
- Saves lives
- Improves lives
- Makes them or their children smarter with tips
- Makes them look better
- Makes them feel better

TV producers need to be able to write and speak a good "tease" for your story in less than 10 seconds. A good exercise is to read some magazine covers and see all the promises or teases luring you to buy:

> *Lose 5 Pounds In A Week!*
> *Save 50 Dollars On Your Next Grocery Bill*

Short, but powerful, promises for the anchors to read before the commercial break keep viewers sticking around to see how we deliver on the promise.

And we *MUST* deliver because if viewers don't get what they've been waiting for, they won't be happy and we've broken their trust.

Thinking of a good tease or promise for the audience is an excellent way to start formulating your pitch. The process will also make you realize the steps you need to take to deliver the segment you're promising.

As with any assignment, you should constantly be thinking about why you are doing the work, and for whom. Know your audience and what they need.

V IS FOR VISUALS

Visuals are so important! This topic really deserves its own chapter. Television is not radio. It's a visual medium. You must show, touch, and reinforce your message with video or graphics.

Think about how viewers will best process your information. For example, while you're talking about how you started the company, we are seeing pictures or video of the company's beginnings. Maybe the visual is the empty lot where you built your factory, or maybe it shows you in the kitchen making a batch of your famous fudge before the bestselling bites ever hit the stores.

People like people. Use visuals to help the audience get to know you.

Remember this key point: In-studio segments are short. You must get your "this is me" elevator pitch down to 20 seconds or less.

Video should support what you're saying and, if the montage is done right, it should keep a viewer glued to the screen.

Don't forget that the viewer is most likely someone yelling at her kids to put their shoes on and scrambling to get off to work. (Personal problem. ☺)

You must be clever to keep the viewer's attention.

Doing a Product Demonstration on "Live" TV

A product demonstration is your chance to shine, but is your widget suited for television? The size of your product matters, and you must think about time too.

Think of the Home Shopping Network. Most of the products promoted there are clothes, jewelry, make-up, or cleaning supplies—items that are easily carried and can fit into a television studio.

How long does your demonstration take? You'll usually have only 3 to 4 minutes to do your thing. If showing off your product takes longer, think about where in the process you can start.

If you're thinking, "Hey, I provide a service. I don't have anything to demonstrate." Really?

Perhaps you're too close to your tricks of the trade and you don't find them amazing anymore. Look around.

That's what my friends Ann Matuszak and Mollie Bartelt thought when I coached them about how to broadcast their photo organizing business, called Pixologie.

I was blown away by their super-fast photo scanner—especially since most of us think photo scanning can only be done one picture at a time. That's precisely why our photos are still in chaos or in shoeboxes. The Pixologie Kodak E-Z Photo scanner pumps out 85 pictures a minute! You can either pay them to scan your pictures or rent the high-speed machine yourself.

My first informal media coaching session.

The Speedy photo scanner, which handled 85 pictures per minute, was the highlight for viewers.

I was sold and I knew the audience would be too. Ann and Mollie nailed the demonstration on TV.

WHAT CAN YOU DEMONSTRATE?
If your demo takes longer than 30 seconds to a minute, can you tell people what you've done so far and then finish off with the awesome results?

Chefs always make the finished meal "just in case." Often, certain products take hours to see the results.

For instance, I once tested a product that was supposed to make just about anything waterproof. You spray the surface of an item and let the liquid dry for 30 minutes, then repeat the process with a top coat.

Obviously, no one wants to watch paint dry, so we shot a video of me spraying suede boots *before* I did the ultimate test of pouring water on them.

We showed the procedure video and then came back "live" in the studio, where we built up the drama and said "Let's see if it really does what it promises." Cue me pouring a pitcher of water over the boots, and the water repelling and landing in a container below. It worked!

Unfortunately, the spray went on white instead of clear and it changed the color of the boots dramatically. It lost me as a potential customer and probably the rest of the audience, too, unless they were going to use it on white sneakers.

It's vital that your product works on live TV. It might work 9 times out of 10, but if it fails on the "Magic Box," your show is over.

WHAT ABOUT PRODUCT DEMONSTRATIONS ON VIDEO?
When I was taking questions after my talk with the "A Woman's Journey" group of entrepreneurs, one woman stood up and told me she had a great business converting real bathtubs into walk-ins for our aging population.

She said her converted tubs cost far less than a whole new walk-in tub. And her tubs don't leak. Of course, we all wanted to *SEE* how she made this happen.

I immediately ruled out doing the demonstration "live" in studio.

First, think size. A bathtub full of water is too big. We don't have water hook-ups in the studio, and setting up a bucket brigade from the kitchen to the studio sounds like a story in itself.

And what if her bathtub actually failed and leaked on TV?

Remember, yours won't be the only segment that day and the crew needs to get you in and out as soon as possible.

So, how could we SEE her converted bathtub? She had to get video of it in action. Keep in mind, most likely, the station will not send a video crew to your location, even if you've been booked for an upcoming segment. Staff is limited and used for hard news stories, not feature stories.

Depending on your budget, your next step would be to hire a professional videographer or ask your teenage kids to use their phones to take a video and do their best work. There are many videos online about how to shoot and edit video. They'll probably rock it.

For example, if the bathtub lady really wants to get the producer's attention, she could send in a 20-second before-and-after video that's funny and has some action. Let's see Grandpa in a beach hat and swimming trunks carrying a cocktail into his walk-in bathtub, seemingly saying he doesn't have a care in the world now.

First, doing the video in a fun way will keep the audience's attention. Would you rather watch a funny Grandpa or a plain bathtub filled with water?

Second, the audience needs to see how the tub performs when someone is actually using it.

Who knows? Grandpa's performance could go viral and you'll get even more attention.

If you are shooting before-and-after video, it's got to be quick. You're only going to get about 3 to 4 minutes to talk during the "live" segment. For the station to produce the show with correct timing, the video should last only about 30 seconds.

* * * * *

TV Insider Lingo for Visuals

To keep the TV screen images changing and the audience entranced with your segment, here are some other insider secrets you should know.

Below are some TV terms to help in pitching your segment idea. You don't have to use this lingo, but if the producer or host starts throwing these words around, at least you'll know what they mean.

- **B-Roll:** That is just video. We will usually need a video of the product, the manufacturing process, and/or the location. We call it "B-roll," because when we edit a story, we have two tracks. The voice or sound goes on track A, and the video is put on track B. If you want a laugh, just google, "We got that B-roll."

- **Billboard:** A billboard is a full-screen graphic that allows you to make bullet points. Usually the title and the subtitle are in all caps, and the bullet points are upper and lower case. Example:

CONSUMER NEWS
TIPS FOR MAKING STRONG PASSWORDS

- Use words plus symbols and numbers
- Don't use 1234 or 0000
- Don't always use the same passwords
- Use 8 or more characters

- **C.G.:** You might be asked, "What do you want for your C.G.?" That stands for "Chyron Generator," which is the software we use to put your name and title on the lower third of the screen while you're talking.

    Your C.G. can't be long, so even if your title is "Supreme Queen of All Things," skip the title. A smart marketer makes sure the name of the company/or product is on the screen. You want people to see the name of what you want them to buy or remember.

- **Full Screen:** This is the full-screen graphic used to show people the name of your company and where they can buy the product or find the service. If you have a logo you'd like to get on screen, ask for a full screen. For the graphics department to make the picture look good, the best format is a JPEG and the file should be no smaller than 600 by 400. Bigger is better. 1920 x 1080 pixels at 72 dots per inch (DPI) is ideal.

- **Package:** This is what we call a reporter's story. All the pieces are edited together like a package. Complete with B-roll video, reporter's voice track, and interviews done—hopefully with you.

- **S.O.T. / Sound On Tape:** S.O.T. is pronounced like the word "sought." This is someone being interviewed on tape, not "live." Maybe it's someone giving testimonials about how great your product is, or perhaps it's a person asking about how the product works and why. For example, a "random" citizen says, "Oh, I haven't seen this before. This would be great for my parents. They would love a walk-in tub. Does it work?"

- **Soundbite:** Sound bites are generally 10- to 15-second interview clips done with other people/experts and then edited into the package.

- **Standup:** The reporter is talking on camera usually "standing up" and doing a demonstration or explaining what's happening.

- **Track:** The reporter lays down a voice track to be edited as part of the package.

- **V.O. / Video Over:** You or the anchors talk over the video. The video's natural sound is very low. This could be video of your facility, the product being made, or the product on the shelves of area stores. Think about what you want to show.

- **V.O. / S.O.T.:** This means video plus sound. Instead of saying Vee-Oh, now we say VO, like "dough." We're running a Vough/Sought.
  Maybe the VO/SOT is a video of the latest medical procedure and an interview with a patient

who loves the results. This is a great way to enhance a live interview with the surgeon on set. The V.O. shows the procedure, and the S.O.T. comes from the patient who is feeling great.

Now you know some tricks to truly producing a TV segment that will keep your audience engaged. Your pitch was AWESOME and you've been BOOKED!

Let's stay with the example of walk-in tubs. To create the "Hook," the company owner should provide the TV producer with information about our aging population, how many are upgrading their homes to stay in them longer, and why her walk-in tubs make life safer and more affordable. Plus, don't forget that awesome video of the crazy, fun Grandpa.

For example, ask yourself:

- Do I have video of my facility or something I want to show off?
- Do I have talking points I want to reinforce by using bullet points on the screen?
- Viewers (potential customers) are going to want to know (using the tub example):
    - What does this service cost?
    - How long does the process take to convert my tub? Or how long will I be without a tub?
    - And does this conversion work on every tub?

I told the owner she needed to give the producer these questions for the host to ask, but if she really wanted to do a great "producing" job, she should also share the answers with them.

Ask the producer if a "full-screen" or a "billboard" would help highlight the answers for the viewers. Of course, the producer makes the final decision on the overall look.

The owner could provide viewers with an example:

**KAREN'S CARPENTRY
CONVERT TO WALK-IN BATHTUB**

- $200 to $400 dollars depending on size
- One week to complete
- Works on every tub except cast iron

Full- screens are also very helpful if you have an event coming up and viewers need to know the date, time, and cost of the event. Usually the station will provide a link to your information on its website.

COMPANY INFO AND LOGO

If you're smart, you'll also provide your company's logo with contact information, just in case the graphics department needs to put your logo into the graphic. Again, you can email a larger JPEG for the best on-air quality, which goes the same for any pictures you provide.

You'd like to see your logo and contact info in a full screen at the end of the segment, but remember, you didn't pay for a commercial. If the producer decides to use your logo—great!

If the producer says, "No, we don't do company logo full-screens at the end of the segment," then say, "No problem. I really appreciate the exposure and being able to share the information with your audience." You want to be asked back.

When you send in your email inquiry, be sure your email has all your contact information, because most likely the station will put your website address on its "links" web page. After all, the station will get some extra web traffic from viewers looking for your information.

There are some other ways you can get your company name on the screen too, but you need to do it the right way.

Once we had a woman come in with a tablecloth full of her company's logo. One well-sized logo in front would have been smart; having 50 medium-sized logos was like someone had thrown up on our display table.

Then to top it off, she put up two logo flag banners to stand at the ends of the table.

The producer didn't have time to ask her to take the banners down and remove the tablecloth. The company rep probably thought she blasted her message out there well, but the look was busy and distracting. I believe the viewers were overwhelmed. She also damaged her relationship with the producer by not asking what was acceptable.

When it comes to dressing your display table, remember less is more. A simple sign on the edge of the table or perhaps propping up your book if you're an author would be appropriate. For example, "On a diet? Let Chef Foster Deadman help."

Chef Foster Deadman—Example of a long table display with subtle US Foods logo (on the football at right).
(Photo courtesy of Fox6now.com)

This is your chance to make your company shine; start thinking about how you can make your product and your display area look appealing.

It's vital to work with producers to tell them how much stuff you'll be bringing. The producer has several different table options and they have to order which one will work best for the crew to know what to roll in.

If you have just a few products, like a new cosmetic line, tell the producer how much space you'll think you'll need. The table should look the right size with no gapping spaces and if you can add pops of color with tablecloths or even cool placements, DO it.

Act like you're having guest over and you're sprucing up the place. Make your display attractive.

Now let's start thinking about—YOU!

Example of a small table with risers to properly display products.
(Photo courtesy of Fox6now.com)

E is for "Engaging"

Being in the studio is amazing. Robotic cameras are moving all around and the lights are bright. *Oh, God, you're about to be on TV!*

Then someone in a hooded sweatshirt (the studio is usually chilly) says, "This is a wireless mic. Just take the cord and run it up under your shirt and I'll attach the clip to your collar."

But the cord is attached to a metal box. Right when you are about to ask, "What do I do with this box?" the person says, "If you have a waistband, slide it on the back or put it in a pocket."

Note to self: Wear something to make this doable and easy. (Detailed instructions coming soon.)

Are you starting to sweat a little? Are you wondering if you're the right person to push your product or service or event on TV, because simply reading about the experience right now is making you nervous?

Don't worry.

Lean into the fear. I tell my son (and myself) that it's good to admit you're afraid. Talk to your fear. Say something like, "Hello, Fear. I'm afraid of you and I'm going to jump on top of you and pound you down…or tickle you."

Hopefully, one of those statements will work for you, or you may have your own method.

Doing anything for the first time is always scary. Just remember how great you'll feel when you nail the interview and your product and/or information is blasted inside the homes of so many people.

GETTING THERE
The first hurdle you will face is saying to others that you want to be on TV. You may have been thinking about going on camera for quite some time, knowing you have information to share, but saying your desire out loud might seem like bragging.

You might be afraid people you care about will say, "Why do you think *YOU* can be on TV? What makes you special?"

I know. I had those thoughts too. Get over this fear because your competitor will, and then run right past you, leaving you in the dust.

The people who care about you should want the best for you. I believe pushing ourselves beyond our comfort zones and taking in as many new experiences as possible is why we were put on this planet.

Maybe once the naysayers see you're taking the risk, they will push themselves in amazing ways too.

Let it go and go for it.

You've probably heard, "Your thoughts become your words, your words become your actions, your actions become your choices, and your choices became your life." I know this to be true. Make choices to benefit you.

How are your thoughts? Are they immediately negative? Are you fearful of television producers and the hosts? Do you mask your fear with excuses like, "Well, they're probably not looking for my type anyway, so why put out all this effort?"

Or do you think, "Making the pitch and producing the segment will take some work, but at least I'll have my ducks in a row when opportunity knocks."

You have the ability to broadcast your business to thousands of people at once; you have to be willing to ask for the opportunity.

What's the saying? Courage is not the absence of fear, but the triumph over it. Be brave and trust yourself. *YOU CAN DO THIS!*

You must have chutzpah! You must ramp up the energy! I mean crazy, MASCOT-type energy!!! With more exclamation marks than you need in normal life!!!!!!

When he was in college, my good friend and anchorman Ted Perry, was Bucky Badger, the mascot for the University of Wisconsin–Madison. He said the best advice he was given before putting on the costume was to go over-the-top with his gestures and antics. This works for TV too.

Bucky Badger mascot (not Ted Perry here).
(Photo from Grantland)

Your voice and your gestures have to be bigger than life. Somehow the "Magic Box" has a way of shrinking down what you do and say. If you talk quietly or without energy, you're going to seem dead, and the segment will die too.

How to Create Energy

When I started out on TV in West Virginia, I was a fast-talking Californian who needed to be slowed down. My news director had me practice my delivery by stretching 30 seconds of copy to a full minute. Pure torture.

Through the years, I've worked with other consultants who have shown me how to be conversational and make sure the viewers can process what I'm saying. I can coach you on this too.

When you're preparing to go on air, you need to use volume, inflection, and pauses to name a few tricks. Trust me, speed does not convey energy.

Often, talking too fast shows you're nervous, and talking too slow can be boring. I can help you practice finding a happy medium.

We can also work on varying your speed, highlighting certain words, and taking small pauses where you want to create a little drama.

Being good on TV takes practice. I'm here if you need me.

The most important tool you need to sharpen is volume. My normal voice and my on-air voice are dramatically different, simply because I raise my volume.

Raising your volume doesn't mean yelling; rather, your voice needs to fill the room. You need to act like you're in an auditorium without a microphone, and you care enough about the people in the back to make sure they can hear you.

You must put yourself out there and act like you're somebody, and you ARE. Remember, you're the one with all the awesome information. You're the person who the host and the producer are relying on to bring BIG and BEAUTIFUL energy to the segment.

Is high energy your normal nature? Answer honestly, because to be good on TV, you must be yourself. You must be authentic. Viewers can tell if you're faking it.

Check yourself right now. Are you saying, "Bring it ON!" or are you hiding under the covers thinking about all those eyeballs watching you?

OVERCOMING THE FEAR
With anything new, the first time is always scary. It's better to say to yourself, "Yep, this is dang scary" and then get on with the show.

In my early days, doing anything new on TV made my stomach hurt and my throat tighten. I would pray and tell myself the experience wasn't going to kill me and if it did kill me, well then, I would get to meet Jesus and that would be okay. Imagine your worst fear coming true, how you would have to deal with the outcome no matter what. And then JUMP!

You'd be okay even if you were so nervous you threw up on live television. Actually, you'd be GREAT! Think about the millions of people who would see the "puking" interview once the video goes viral. You might even be invited on national talk shows and late-night shows to talk about what happened.

Of course, not the outcome you want, but you can always spin a bad situation into a positive one.

Again, "tickling" the fear calms me down.

Another quick example: When I knew I'd be interviewing then Senator John Kerry, who was running for President in 2004, I was nervous. People think the person being interviewed is worried about giving a dumb answer; well, guess what? Journalists are worried about asking stupid questions.

My dad called earlier in the day and asked if I was nervous. I told him, "Yes, but when Kerry walks up to me, I'm going to think about one of my favorite jokes."

Joke:
A horse walks into a bar.
Bartender says, "Why the long face?"

Please tell me you get my sense of humor.

Remember—just have fun.

Today, when I am about to interview someone, and I can see a little fear, I ask, "Are you nervous?"

Usually the person says, "Yes, a little."

I reply with, "Terrific. Enjoy the buzzing feeling. Being nervous means you truly care, which shows you're going to be great. You're the expert. You've got this."

Most people smile and realize those words are true. They shine when the camera comes on.

If you are not an outgoing person by nature, and you're still about to puke just reading my pep talk here, why put yourself through the aggravation?

Your organization must put its best foot forward, and your foot might not be the wise choice. If you're not feeling "it," think about other people in your company who would be good. Who is likeable and likes to talk? Who smiles a lot and always makes people happy to be around them? Who is great about relaying information people can understand?

That is the person you need to put in front of the camera if he or she can also pass the "What does the person look like?" test. As shallow as this test might seem, television viewers are quick to judge a person's appearance.

Engaging Personalities LOOK the Part

We've talked about visuals and dressing up your product/service for TV, but how are we going to dress YOU up?

Being on television is a performance! Go directly to the Wardrobe Department for your costume. Except local television stations don't have a wardrobe department. They hope you do.

If you're a firefighter or police officer, please wear your uniform. If you're a doctor or a nurse, please wear your lab coat or your scrubs.

You might think coming in a suit or dress is more professional, but your work clothes instantly show the audience what you do. Viewers might even turn up the volume once they see someone of importance is on the screen.

Think of Professor Maria from *Mad Science*. ALL of us wear the science costume/lab coats and goggles when she's on. The look is "fun," even for the Production Coordinator. ☺

You can't help but laugh and learn while watching Professor Maria's segments.
(Photo courtesy of Fox6now.com)

Before viewers can like your product or your service, they have to like YOU, the presenter. Most people make the decision fast. Don't you?

A consultant told me people take less than 7 seconds to decide if they like your hair, your clothes, your makeup. THEN they decide whether to listen to you.

Can you or the perfect representative of your company conquer the 7-second test? *Absolutely!*

You simply have to practice getting across the right message with the right look.

Let's get truly superficial for a second because television is.

A presenter doesn't have to be ultra-attractive, but he or she should be attractive to the key demographic for your product.

Case in point: Bree Schumacher is a mother who promoted healthy, low-cal recipes for the whole family through her blog, Skinny Mommy. Some of the recipes included sauces she sells at a few local markets. Her business wouldn't work as well if she wasn't slender. I'm just being honest.

The first time Bree came on our show, she was one of several guests. The local technical college was doing a contest for local entrepreneurs. Right away, I could see she had the "IT" factor.

She was bubbly and infused tons of energy into the discussion. She also had great products with her mixing sauces. After we were done and all the guests were walking off the set, I asked her if she'd be interested in doing a cooking segment for us. She said yes. The producer of the show agreed and decided to give her a shot.

Sure, the first cooking session wasn't her best appearance since she didn't finish the dish before the segment was over, but she came back again and again and nailed it.

WHAT TO WEAR ON AIR

While your personality needs to be bright, your clothes need to be bright too. In the biz, we say you need to POP—but don't explode!

Solid jewel-tone colors are best like bright blue, green, orange, yellow, and red. Watch what the hosts are wearing.

If you wear stripes or busy prints, you could become a mesmerizing mess and no one will listen to a thing you're saying. They'll be either hypnotized by your stripes or turn the channel instead.

Next, don't wave the white flag! If you wear a white shirt, the cameras have a hard time reading the brightness and they will retreat, meaning that the

Stripes or busy prints are a "no-no" for TV.

camera operator will have to adjust the iris in the camera lens and dim the whole look of your presentation.

It's all right to wear a white shirt under a suit jacket because white in small amounts won't affect the cameras. A beige or cream-colored top can still work, depending on the studio. Always feel free to ask the producer what is best.

Makeup

Okay, so what are you going to wear on your face? Both men and women need to wear makeup.

Guys, put on a light foundation first and then cover your entire face with a light powder, especially your forehead and near your hairline because once you get a little nervous (and you will), you'll want to block any sweat that form and conceal any redness.

If you're saying, "There's no way I'm wearing makeup," at least put on some powder to cut down the shine.

People need to trust you. You don't want viewers to think you're selling snake oil and you put a few drops on your face.

Ladies, your makeup should be professional and don't be afraid to put on more than normal. Double it. Yes, double! Trust me, the studio lights will wash you out. If you're really concerned about how you look, the cheapest way to get the look you'd like is to ask a friend who is good at doing makeup to come with you and polish you up before your performance. You can also pay for a professional makeup artist by either asking around for a recommendation or going to Thumbtack, which is a freelancer's site.

Big-time media markets like New York, L.A., and Chicago will have makeup artists. Their producers should let you know if your makeup will be done by their artist. Some stations might even tell you what time to be there for makeup.

If they don't mention it, ask. However, in most local markets, know that you're on your own.

ON AIR — BROADCAST YOUR BUSINESS

Financial expert Nick Foulks—the picture of dressing for success.
(Photo courtesy of Fox6Now.com)

WOULD I BUY FROM THAT GUY?

Take a good hard look at your overall appearance and ask yourself, "Would I buy from me or my representative?" People need to trust the presenter and in some ways, the viewer should want to be like them.

For example, Nick Foulks is a financial expert. The quality of his suit and tie scream, "Dang, I'm good with money. You should listen to me."

Take a couple of days to pick out the right clothes, make-up and hairstyle to pass your 7-second test.

Now let's start thinking about what you are going to say for the remainder of your 3 to 5 minutes on air.

ENGAGING WORDS

In my experience, most of the time, a guest will come into the studio and, quite frankly, act like a guest—which would be the proper way to act in almost all situations except on television.

Why? On television, you need to lead the program's host. You've already started the process by producing your own segment with the producer.

When interacting with the host, don't limit yourself by answering his or her questions with a few simple words. That type of stilted conversation is awkward to watch and puts a great deal of pressure on the host to fill the allotted time and keep the viewers watching.

Expand on your answers, take the conversation in fun directions and engage the host with some questions of your own.

Understandably, first-timers will be nervous, and since they don't know what to expect, they will allow the host to lead the presentation. Don't do this!

You must take control and help the host though YOUR segment. I can't say this enough. Once the host introduces you and explains to the viewers what you're cooking up for them, YOU MUST BECOME THE LEADER!

The hosts' mind is busy with other topics and news of the day. He or she won't have your segment mastered like you do. Most likely, the host is reading through your information in the commercial break before you come on.

Are you really going to let someone who knows very little about your business control your destiny and the destiny of your organization or business?

NO!

To figure out what you want to say, first think about what you want the viewers to remember.

Answer these overview questions:

- "What do I want the viewers to know about me?" Remember, people like people.
- "What can I teach to save them time/money and make their lives better?"
- "What do I want them to realize about how my product or service can help?"
- "What action would I like them to take?"

Your answers should reveal:

- a likable story about you
- what you can teach people
- why doing business with you will help them
- why they should buy your product or service, or go to the event

You get the picture.

You've probably heard about the KISS method. "Keep It Simple, Stupid"…or in my version, "Sweetie." This rule was made for TV—and for talking to your husband while he's watching a sporting event. ☺

Viewers could be making a meal, corralling their kids, who knows what, and if your message gets complicated, they'll tune out and you've lost a customer.

Even though you might love imparting tons of industry-insider lingo to show your brilliance, get over yourself and break down your message for the rest of us. You'll be more effective.

THE SHORTEST FIVE MINUTES OF YOUR LIFE

Next, how much time is the producer giving you for your segment? You've likely heard of the 20-second elevator speech, in which you can precisely tell someone about your skills in a chance meeting with a CEO on the elevator. Now you're going to get more time.

When you're booked on a morning or afternoon talk show, usually you will have between 3 to 5 minutes to get across information about your product, service and mission. The timing all depends on how many segments and stories the producer has planned for that day, and when the commercial breaks need to be hit.

You might think a few minutes will be more than enough, but when the red lights of the cameras go on, you're about to experience the fastest few minutes of your life.

I can't tell you how many guests have looked at me afterwards and said, "Wow, that went fast! I didn't even get to say everything I had planned."

The lesson here: **Make your key points right away.**

GIVE THEM THE QUESTIONS TO ASK AHEAD OF TIME

Most anchors or hosts already know what questions to ask you, but providing them with questions ahead of time will make everyone more comfortable. The hosts may not use the questions you brought, but at least they'll know what you are prepared to answer.

Once you've been booked, email the producer with your "host questions." Simply take your talking points and turn them into questions so you can knock the answers out of the park.

- Why did you come up with this idea?
- Who is this event for?

People need to know a little about you and why you saw the need for this product or service.

- Can you show me how it works?

Remember, this is your time to shine. Smile and walk the host through how it works. Don't be afraid to share some of the trials and things that have gone wrong along the way. It makes you human and likeable.

- How much does the product or service cost? Tell the host and the audience why it's such a great value.
- Where can people get it?
- How can people get in touch with you?

Tell the host and the viewers. Remember to ask the producer if it's possible to put a link to your website on the station's website. The host should also be able to mention that all the information is available on the station's website.

Do Some Research on Your Host

Don't be afraid to be playful with the host during the segment. In fact, you'd be wise to know a little about all of the show hosts since you won't know which one is assigned to your segment until you get there. All of their bios should be on the station's website.

Having some knowledge about them, or the show, will make them instantly like you because you'll come across as a fan. The audience will feel like you're one of them.

For example, "Kim [*the host*], I know with three kids at home, you are a busy lady and this new dinner starter kit would be perfect for you."

"John [*the host*], if you want to impress some ladies by cooking dinner at your home, I'm just saying [*smile*], this dinner starter kit would be perfect for you."

The audience likes to be entertained and if you're entertaining them, while at the same time, selling your product or message, then you're generating real clients.

"Where Do I Look?"
Before we go on air, the most common question I'm asked is, "Where do I look? At you or the camera?"

Today, before my guests can even get the words out, I deliver instructions like the nurse who tells all her patients which way the gown should face so their backsides don't show.

When I was the host, I said, "The trick to being on TV is to look at me, because we are just having a conversation. Forget the cameras are even there."

When you're on air, the host will introduce you looking directly at the camera. This one-on-one eye contact with the viewers is reserved for the host. If you try talking directly with the viewers, you're not giving the host the proper respect. In addition, the producer might think you're trying to do a full-blown commercial and not invite you back.

You can glance at the camera/viewers with a *QUICK* nod to say, "I know you're there and you're important," but this move takes some practice.

TIME'S UP
In my experience, while some guests might be nervous, others can't get enough of the camera and the adrenaline rush.

No matter how much you're loving the spotlight, please realize when your scene is over—don't go past the allotted segment time. When you feel the host wrapping things up, *DO NOT* try to get in one more quick statement.

News programs are carefully timed out, and your extra 15- or 30-second plug now has the producer scrambling to figure out what story to drop, or what segment to shorten to make up the time.

Don't be a time hog! If you keep talking beyond your allotted time, the host will be forced to cut you off in an awkward or rude way. You don't want to be that person. You want to be invited back! Follow the host/anchor's lead, listen to when the segment is drawing to a close, thank the host—and stop talking.

Before you ever go on air, practice with a stop watch. Have a friend play the host, get in some playful banter and see how long the segment will run.

Television shows are like life—the only constant is change.

The producer told you the segment would run 3 minutes, and you have your presentation down to 3 minutes on the dot. When you arrive, you're told your segment has been cut to 2 minutes or that you need to fill 4 minutes.

The timing all depends on what happened earlier in the show. The smart guest (*YOU!*) will simply smile and say, "No problem," even though your brain is screaming, "I haven't practiced cutting the presentation down" or "I'm not sure how to expand it."

To this, I say, "Let go and use 'The Force,' Luke." In other words, go with the flow.

The segment you practiced was merely a fantasy anyway. When you're in the real game, the plays never work out perfectly. Thankfully, all the practice has given you a solid foundation of knowing you're prepared, no matter what happens.

The trick is remembering your first appearance hopefully won't be your last. If you're good, there's a chance of being an "occasional guest" or even a "regular." A regular is someone who has a product or service that keeps on giving, such as a local chef with a great personality and a cookbook full of yummy recipes.

Like Amy Hanten, "The Cooking Mom." She knows how to dish up some audience benefit, poke a little fun at the host, and deliver her message.

Of course, she's a pro after years of being a morning TV anchor and now hosting her own cooking show in Green Bay. She seamlessly works a little promotion into her performance.

When I think of an occasional guest, I think of a gift-shop owner highlighting great gifts for all the different holidays, or a professional organizer who is going to tackle the kid's closet's just in time to start school, or battle the overflowing garage so the family is able to get the cars in for the winter. Always be thinking of ways to update your pitch.

Keep bringing what you **H.A.V.E.** again and again. When producers know you have "IT," you can truly make their jobs easier.

Amy Hanten, The Cooking Mom
(Photo courtesy of Fox6Now.com)

NOTES

Chapter 3
BEING BOOKED AS AN EXPERT!

Okay, so you don't have a product. Instead, you have a service or an area of expertise and want to share your information with the public. How do you get on the radar for news reporters and producers to call you?

I'll explain, but first, these are the experts often called upon to share their knowledge:

- Attorney
- Car Improvement/Maintenance
- Consumer Expert/Better Business Bureau
- Doctor
- Dietician
- Financial Expert
- Home Improvement/Maintenance
- Military or Aviation Expert
- Psychologist
- Political Analyst

- Professional Organizer
- Social Media Expert
- Technology Expert

... just to name a few. Usually, being chosen for an interview depends on the topic of the day and how much your information will benefit the viewer. If you think your expertise would help inform the public, reach out.

Usually the media chooses experts who are affiliated with a trade industry association, college, or hospital group. The media like to know you have the backing from another organization and that someone else has already "signed off" on you. If you don't have an affiliation yet, go get involved.

If you already are a trade expert, industry leader, professor, doctor, or other specialist, think about how much clout or prestige being a regular guest or go-to person for local media will give you.

Perhaps your organization has public relations people who know the hosts/reporters/producers and can make the calls to get you booked. Typically, the PR person is the go-between. However, once you've met the reporter/producer, it's up to you to keep the relationship alive.

Reporters and anchors like to have "sources." They like their bosses to know they have people throughout the community sending in ideas and information. Become that person, that "expert" for the station and we could be scratching each other's backs for years to come.

Simply shoot the host or anchor an email once a month or call every couple of months to check in. Especially contact the station when you have a nugget of information to share.

TIME IT RIGHT

If you're going to call, know our deadlines or "crunch" times. Nothing puts you in the "annoying" category like the person who calls to chat an hour before our deadline. Usually it's best to call reporters and producers at the beginning of their shifts.

For a 9-to-5 ("day-side") reporter, the best time to call would be between 10 and 11 a.m. A "night-side" reporter is best contacted around 2:30 to 3:30 p.m., because that's when they start.

If you're calling producers, you need to know when their show starts and call 5 hours before then.

Once you have a media person on the line, ask if it's a good time for that person, and establish when the person likes to be contacted.

When there's a hot topic in the news and you're the expert the media needs, capitalize on the moment and call immediately. Let's say you're a life coach and a new study just came out about the high percentage of people who won't ask for a raise. Now is your time to call the producer to say, "I have three tips to help your viewers learn how to effectively negotiate."

The "Hook" is the new study.

Or what if there is a new virus outbreak and we need a doctor to explain to the public how to prevent the disease and how to spot the symptoms? If you've created a relationship with the reporter/producer, then you'll be the one to fill the slot when it's show time.

Often, the opportunity isn't clear cut and you'll need to spin or maneuver your expert opinion into the mix.

Pay Attention to What's Happening in the World

For instance, there's been a shooting. The person who pulled the trigger has a concealed-carry permit and claims he had to use his gun in self-defense. The reporter knows all of this because it's written in the police report and criminal complaint. While the information is great, the police aren't talking.

None of the neighbors where the shooting occurred want to talk on camera and the shooter's family is hiding from the live TV trucks surrounding their house.

In TV news, the reporter needs "sound bites." A story with *just* the reporter's voice does not make a good story. If we don't have people to talk with us on camera, we're simply reading a criminal complaint to the viewers, which they can do themselves online.

If you own a gun shop, or are the leader of a local gun club or a national concealed-carry association, now is your time. You don't have to talk about the specifics of the case. In fact, you shouldn't. However, if you're smart, you can get your general message out there.

As the expert, you could provide answers to these possible questions:

- What laws "could" be considered in this case?
- What does the "stand-your-ground law" really cover?
- How might the shooter be protected by having a permit?
- What is some general information about the gun listed in the criminal complaint?
- Why is this gun a popular model? Or why isn't it?
- How far will the bullet travel?

When you give the media an on-camera interview with useful information, you are now the EXPERT in our story. Even though the reporter may not have been able to obtain the much-desired emotional, "I can't believe this happened here," neighborhood angle, your knowledge and expertise will really benefit the audience.

When reporters are in a bind and you're always at the ready, expect your phone to ring. Do a good job in the interview, and reporters will come back to you because you've made their jobs easier.

If we call with only a couple hours to our deadline and you say," Sure, I can talk," or "Sure, I'll set up something for you," you now are on speed-dial for the media and free publicity.

News is constantly changing and your expertise could make a difference. Be ready and flexible.

I can't tell you the number of people who just aren't ready or can't make the interview happen. Maybe their business doesn't move as quickly as the "What do you have for me right now?" news business. However, if I owned a business or was leading an organization and a TV station called me up, I'd say, "You betcha. Free publicity. I'm in."

BE BOOKED AS AN EXPERT

RECORDED INTERVIEWS WITH EXPERTS

Reporters with daily deadlines are the ones who usually need you fast. That's a whole different ball game than being booked for a show. The reporter and a photojournalist (cameraman/camerawoman) will most likely come to you. They will interview you for maybe 15 minutes, then say thank you and leave.

Most likely, they will interview a few other people before returning to the station, reviewing the video, determining which were the best answers, and then writing and editing the story for a later broadcast.

You know how politicians don't ever seem to answer questions thrown at them? While annoying, they are masters at getting their message across. Practice saying the points you want to make and then peppering them throughout your actual responses.

Usually reporters will choose only one or two of your best "sound bites," and generally anything more than 15 seconds will get cut. Since your interview is not going to be "live," you may have the chance to time and edit yourself before the camera comes on.

* * * * *

When I was growing up, my mother had her own real estate company with one of her closest friends. They were two empowered women and I was in awe of them, especially when my mom made it on the "Magic Box."

During the energy crisis of the early 1980s, the City Council of Fresno, California, was considering an ordinance to make homes more energy efficient. One of the ideas was to upgrade or retrofit older homes by putting weather-stripping around the doors.

In theory, the plan was great, but would cost home owners a fortune to bring older homes into compliance. The work would have been required before the home was sold.

The trickle-down effect would be that homeowners, especially the elderly, could not sell their homes because they were unable to pay the retrofitting costs.

Since realtors make their money by selling homes, and most are homeowners themselves, the potential ordinance could mean a huge financial blow to the industry.

My mother had heard about the proposal at a morning meeting for real estate brokers, and even though realtors were just finding out, the measure was on the fast-track to be passed.

Suddenly, that afternoon, there was a knock at our door. It was our city councilman. Weird. My mom said that was the first time a politician had ever come to her door. He was campaigning, but she asked him what he knew about the retrofitting ordinance. He said, "Are you for it or against it?"

She said, "I'm against it."

He said, "Okay, I'll come in."

He explained the plan was moving forward fast and was on the agenda to be passed the next week. For him to pull the ordinance off the agenda, she had to do two things.

First, she had to call the media and tell them, "Something big is going to be happening at the City Council meeting." Second, she actually had to deliver a big crowd. Immediately, Mom started calling her colleagues and the TV stations.

They packed the house—their livelihood was at stake. The big crowd grabbed the attention of the media and my mother was interviewed on TV. Later, at the dinner table, she told us a reporter talked with her for about 10 minutes. When we watched the news that evening, she was only on for 20 seconds or less. Whether or not the ordinance was stopped, I thought seeing my mom on the tube was so cool.

For a short period in her life, she became the so-called real estate "expert." (Today, she'll tell you she's an expert in a lot of areas now that she's an attorney.)

* * * * *

Luckily, news stations don't have set "expert requirements." Reporters are always looking for someone who can deliver good information with a lot of personality.

Remember E is for Engaging and being entertaining is the key to being deemed a great expert by both the media and the viewers alike.

While you should still try to have terrific video or a demonstration, usually experts rely on their energy and passion to reach the audience.

Quick Expert Test

Can you smile?
If you answer no, please stop reading and see a doctor. ☺
    We all know smiling makes you instantly more likable. However, sometimes lifting your cheeks can be hard to do when you're nervous. Practice smiling showing teeth and see how long you can hold the pose naturally. You want a calm, in-control smile, as opposed to the "I was told to smile and now I can't bring down my cheeks" look.

Can you be passionate and make the viewers passionate about your subject?
The answer should be an easy "YES," since you naturally love talking about your work or your field

of expertise, and have the enthusiasm to pump up others.

Can you talk in sound bites?
Your answers should be tight and clever since reporters choose sound bites that are 15 seconds or less. We always choose statements which are funny, hit the nail on the head, or moments when you get excited and more passionate.

You need to be the life of the party, because video has a tendency to flatten people out. Just when you think you're pumped up and giving all the energy you have, you'll see the segment and be amazed how normal you come across.

Remember—mascot-crazy-type energy is what will make the audience look up and take notice of you. They turn on the television because they want to see emotion. They want to see memorable moments. They want to feel something.

PULLING OFF A WINNING PERFORMANCE AS AN EXPERT— THE EMOTIONAL OPINION

Now you know what the media is looking for in an expert interview. So how do you pull off a winning performance?

Start thinking of what you'll probably be asked. Then think of the questions you *WANT* to be asked. Come up with great, fun, and quick answers.

Write out your answers, read them out loud, and then time yourself to make sure your responses are 15 seconds or less. Then say them in a conversational way to your friends and family and see how they respond. Do they think your comments are quick, funny, and/or carry some emotion? If they like what you're saying, practice, practice, practice!!

You can do this while you're driving. You can do this sitting at home with your video camera recording. You can do this with a friend feeding you the questions, or I can do a private coaching session with you too.

Keep working on your answers until you combine the perfect amount of feelings with the facts.

Notice I said "feelings" before "facts" because honestly, a good reporter will steal the facts from you and rely on you for the heartfelt opinion. The unbiased media should not have or give an opinion.

Reporters frequently ask the same question in different ways because they're digging for an emotional opinion. Emotion sells and they know if they strike the right cord, you'll sing.

Don't worry about not looking like you have all the facts. Reporters will voice ("track") the information you provide and tell people you're the one who told them. For example:

Be Booked as an Expert

REPORTER: "The Department of Transportation says the freeway will cost 95 gazillion dollars and take 5 years to complete. Nearby businesses aren't happy."

NEARBY BUSINESS WOMAN: "We've been told they'll do all they can to keep the roads open to my store, but honestly I'm devastated. I'll probably have to send up fireworks just to show people I'm still here."

Journalists covering health or technology gravitate to experts who can simplify the procedure or the equipment, and emotionally explain why a breakthrough is so amazing.

Again, as in the case of being on live TV, take ownership of the interview, have your facts prepared but, more importantly, be ready to release memorable sound bites. Once you are good at delivering with emotion, we reporters will keep coming back and your bosses and/or clients will love it.

Live Interviews with an Expert

Let's say you're considered an expert and the station has just booked you for a "live" shot or "live" talk-show interview. Breathe a sigh of relief. ☺

"*What?!? It's going to be live? Why would I be relieved?*"

You now have the great opportunity of being in front of potential customers for a couple of minutes instead of a couple of seconds—and you can't be edited. Everything you say will be broadcast in real time to the viewers. You don't have to worry about giving a small bite, so be prepared to give a mouthful.

Number-one rule: **Don't bore the audience!** When the host asks you a question, your answer can be longer than 15 seconds, but if you drone on for too long (25 seconds), the audience will lose interest.

TV stations pay for minute-by-minute research to show when viewers tune out. To keep viewers watching, we've learned that video and sound need to keep changing. If you go on too long without the host having the chance to chime in, this means the sound hasn't changed and the audience will hit the remote. Remember, viewers want and expect to watch a conversation.

Think of the minute-by-minute research as a challenge! Channel-changers will sit in awe of your information or quick presentation, and the station will see the numbers stay steady while you're on the screen. In fact, if producers promote your segment well enough the day before, or with a couple of commercials ahead of your appearance, more people will be tuning in.

You'll be a star! Especially if you keep delivering again and again with new content ideas for the show.

Be Booked as an Expert

Experts can often be boring on a talk show. One-on-one interviews are Snoozeville unless you or your public relations team comes up with clever and well-produced segment ideas. Local television producers don't have the time to craft amazing segments for you. You have to be the producer.

Think about the following:

- What kind of video or demonstration can I show?
- Could I ask the producer for a bullet-point graphic to highlight the key points?
- Could I ask if the host is willing to do a role-playing game?
  Yes, wigs and costumes are acceptable.
- Or could I turn my information into a quiz game?
  That way the viewer and the host are playing along and generally interested in hearing the answers. Ask a couple of true or false questions, or stump the host with a few multiple-choice questions.

Clever + Content = Coverage

Now that you have an idea of how crazy and fun you can make "your" segment, the studio ceiling is the limit!

ON AIR — BROADCAST YOUR BUSINESS

Playing keeps the host and the audience engaged.
(Photo courtesy of Fox6Now.com)

Talking about women and wealth — Let's play a game!
(Photo courtesy of Fox6Now.com)

Chapter 4
HOW TO WRITE A KILLER EMAIL

Sharpen your brain and exercise your fingers because you're about to *write* your way into the hearts of media professionals.

Sure, you could brandish a beautiful, multi-color press kit in front of their faces, but before you do that, why not take a chance with a simple email?

While some companies pay big money to PR firms to write up big releases, you don't have to work so hard. You do, however, really need to know how to write a Killer Email that comes with a great promise and a "shiny" subject line.

I say *shiny* because the subject line is your lure to "Hook" the reader. If this one line is dull or confusing, then your audience is going to swim on by.

Speaking of fish, remember when I told you we were making holiday cocktails using herring on our show? Yuck, right? But the local company had the right "Hook" and gave us a different and fun segment idea for the New Year.

However, we almost didn't book them because this was their subject line:

**INTERVIEW OPPORTUNITY:
HERRING DELIVERY DEC. 13 FROM MA BAENSCH HERRING
FOR GOOD LUCK IN THE NEW YEAR**

First, the words "Interview Opportunity" may pique viewers' interest a bit, but they take up most of the subject line. Depending on the recipient's email layout, the producer might not see any other words.

"Interview Opportunity" must have been sold as the hot new buzz phrase in the PR industry, because many companies nationwide use this phrase in their subject lines. Once anything is overused, it's no longer attractive and TV folks look past the pitch and hit *delete*. The goal here is not to wind up in the trash bin.

Next, who in the TV world would care about a herring delivery on Dec. 13th? I would assume delivery of a herring shipment would be pretty common in the fishing industry and not ***news***worthy.

So why did the station bite? We recognized the name of the local company. Once we were inside the body of the email message, the pitch was great. In the opening line, we were ***promised*** a fun segment for Studio A, complete with how to stir up two unique drinks for the holidays. And to top it off, the owner of the company, Kim Wall, could talk about the tradition of herring as good luck and the health benefits for our viewers. Hooray! They H.A.V.E. what it takes.

- **Hook**: The holidays, and a NEW use for a well-known product
- **Audience Benefit:** Improve your health; Omega 3s are good for you / Improve your life; serve your guests something NEW
- **Visual:** Demonstration, host prepares drink
  Video: Station shot video of local herring packing plant
- **Engaging**: The new owner of the company— the "Ma" in Ma Baensch— was high-energy and funny

The email went on to explain how the company would like to deliver some herring to the station for us to taste this amazing and healthy fish. The delivery was for the station! That certainly wasn't clear in the subject line.

In the end, maybe herring is good luck because luckily, we didn't delete the pitch, and the segment was great.

Ask yourself how to get your promise into the shiny subject line. If I were to rewrite the company's subject line, I'd simply put:

SUBJECT: LET'S MIX UP NEW & HEALTHY HOLIDAY DRINK RECIPES. WE'RE LOCAL. YOU IN?

Make the sentence shine by highlighting with BOLD text the most important selling points.

What are you selling? What's your promise? While continually thinking about what you H.A.V.E. for your segment, keep carving the subject line down until it's 15 words or less.

Once you've "Hooked" the media, your email should deliver the rest of the information and don't forget— less is MORE!

Do you like to read long or short emails? When I see a lot of text, my eyes glaze over. While I might read the email later, you won't receive an immediate response. The longer your words sit there, the greater chance I'll delete them or drag them over to a folder only to be seen much later.

Tell me the who, what, when, and where *quickly*. I've talked to my co-workers about their email preferences too, and everyone tells me any email longer than three short paragraphs runs the risk of being deleted or put on the back burner.

READY FOR A RANT? IT'S EDUCATIONAL ☺

It's so annoying when people send us an email with a decent subject line, but then inside the actual email, there is only one line reading, "Please see the attached press release."

Really? We have not yet been greeted with catchy information and you're asking us to click on an attachment that will most likely be too long to read. Do you really want to take that gamble?

Journalists need a quick scan. We have been trained through the years to hate press releases. The mere mention of this format screams, "Don't waste your time!"

Obviously, I don't recommend old-school press releases, but if you feel you must, at least cut and paste the release ***directly*** into your email.

Also don't ask for a read receipt. The pop-up box is annoying and you don't want to be "that" person. If you really want to know if I've read it, call me or follow up with another email a week later.

Knowing my media colleagues are overwhelmed with email, I came up with this "Killer Email Template" for you to cut through the noise. You can also download it as a PDF on my website at Katrina-Cravy.com

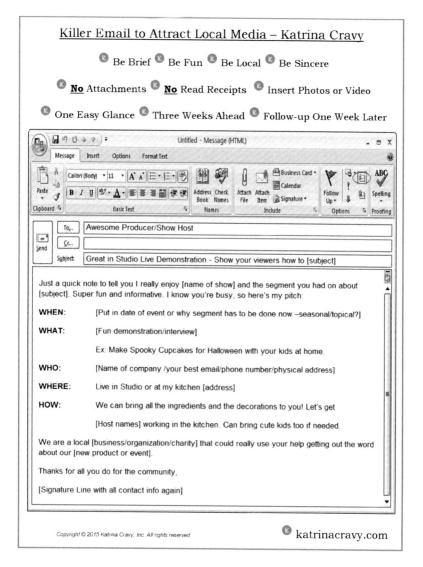

And for my BONUS ROUND of this *Killer Email* chapter, include some added value for the reporter or producer.

Station managers know digital content is the wave of the future and they are asking all employees to up their social media game by posting more often. Honestly, I think doing social media correctly is a full-time job and my time is limited.

If a public relations person adds a potential Twitter or Facebook post I believe is beneficial for my viewers, I'll post your content, especially if you've taken the time to find all the correct Twitter handles and Facebook pages, plus your copy is well written.

Finding the "@InsertCorrectAccountHere" drives me nuts. Most reporters don't have time. For instance, the Lakeshore Chinooks, a local baseball team in the Northwoods League, was offering a family night with discounted tickets and fun activities for kids. Since I'm a mom, baseball lover, and was a consumer reporter, the game is a good deal. I don't mind sharing the offer with

my social media followers if all the work has been done for me.

I know this example looks like I'm asking people to do my job, but honestly, a deal for a night out to watch a local baseball team isn't high on the priority list. Reporters have to work on the stories they've been assigned, which usually affect more viewers.

When I was still doing reporter work, I would hand the information over to the producer to see if this great deal is worth a mention in the show, but if the answer is "no," at least you provided the reporter or host with a potential social media post.

My advice is to include the content in the email and write, "Feel free to use this as a Tweetable or a Facebook Flash to your followers. They'll thank you for it and so will we."

Giving your content a catchy label makes what you're sharing more attractive. Marketing is everything. Then, by having the reporter or TV hosts retweet or share your content on the Facebook page, you gain more creditability and the reporter/host might gain more followers from your fan base.

On-air personalities usually have thousands of people following them on Facebook and Twitter. If they share your "Tweetable" or "Facebook Flash," writing the content for them was well worth your time.

Through emails and calls, you can create a great win-win relationship for you and the reporter/host/producer.

SENDING YOUR KILLER EMAIL TO THE RIGHT PERSON

Who you gonna call? Ghostbusters? (Sorry, I couldn't resist. ☺)

First, decide what you want—a segment in the studio with the TV host asking you questions, or a reporter coming to your place of business?

If you think your pitch is best suited to be a guest on a live show, you need to contact the producer who is in charge of the morning show or the talk show highlighting local businesses.

If you think your story is best told by a reporter who comes to your company, you'll need to first find out which reporter usually covers your topic. For instance, the president of the local Better Business Bureau would contact the consumer reporter.

Generally, reporter titles or areas of specialization are listed on the "team page" of the station's website. Reporters' email addresses may be listed there as well. If not, you're going to need to call the station.

Call the general number and ask the receptionist who handles bookings for the show or the report who usually covers your type of story.

If the receptionist doesn't know, ask to be transferred to the News Assignment Desk. The folks on the

Assignment Desk know everyone's true job, while the station's general receptionist might not.

You see, the Assignment Desk is the heart of the newsroom. The Assignment Editor is the one who reviews all the emails, calls, faxes, and news releases. If a topic or event grabs the Assignment Editor's attention, it could be "assigned" to a reporter.

Assignment editors are usually super busy and might have a quick or gruff demeanor on the phone, so get right to the point. Ask for the name of the reporter or producer for the show, that person's email address and direct phone number.

Then thank the assignment editor profusely and say, "Great! Now I won't have to bug you again. I really appreciate it!"

Once you see the email address pattern, firstname.lastname@station.com, you should be able to email anyone at the station you wish.

You can create a great win-win relationship for you and the reporter/host/producer when you write Killer Emails with terrific content.

CAUTION ALERT! REMINDER ABOUT KILLER EMAILS
Don't send your intro email to everyone at once. Emails copied to everyone don't get the attention they deserve because people aren't sure who is taking the lead.

Don't send the email pitch privately to other people on the team after you've been told "No" or "Not now." The team does talk and they'll have a negative feeling about you for not listening to Daddy and running to Mommy instead.

If you don't get a response at all, you need to attract the media's attention somehow. Wait a couple of months before sending out your next Killer Email.

This time, without becoming a stalker, you need to find out as much as you can about the host, reporter, or producer. You'll get an idea of what floats their boat simply by following them on Twitter and Facebook.

Remember the Skinny Mommy business on how to make quick and healthy meals mentioned above? Bree's business is right in my wheelhouse. I'm a busy mom who wants to make sure my family eats well. She could contact me directly.

Let's say you have a software or tech-type product. Figure out which reporters do the tech stories or seem really interested in showing off their new Apple watch.

Follow the Twitter and Facebook accounts for the TV shows you're interested in appearing on and then chime in with comments. Tell them how much you liked certain segments. Show producers monitor these accounts and creating a small relationship on Twitter or Facebook could give you some name recognition when you send your Killer Email.

Chapter 5

MAKING THE PERFECT PHONE PITCH

"So much for the win-win, Katrina. They're not responding to my Killer Email."

Take a deep breath and remember how often you don't get back to people right away. Life is busy and your agenda and the media's agenda don't always jive.

Did you send a follow-up email saying something like, "Just circling back to make sure you got the email I sent you last week." If you're still only hearing crickets, it's time to MAKE THE CALL.

As much as we all hate cold calling, you MUST take action and make your sales or story pitch. You have the number to call from when you talked to the Assignment Editor.

We all love stories about how an amazing opportunity landed in someone's lap. When we dig deeper, though, we'll often discover the person was in the right place, at the right time, with the right preparation. To be that person, you must step out and say, "Hey!"

Before you make this call, PLEASE, PLEASE prepare what you H.A.V.E. to offer them. Come up with your Hook by giving the people you call a reason you should be on the show NOW, how it will benefit the Audience, your Visuals, and show them on the phone how Engaging you can be.

The worst way to start a conversation is by saying, "Did you get my email?" This question is guaranteed to put the media folks on the defensive because either they don't remember your email, deleted it, or haven't responded yet. They are already feeling bad and don't like getting this kind of phone call.

Once you have your H.A.V.E. ducks in a row, dial up and see if the person has time to answer a quick question.

PERFECT PITCH CONVERSATION EXAMPLE:

As soon as you reach the person you're looking for, launch in and say, "Hi, I'm [YOUR NAME]. I think I have a great idea for your show. I'm following up on an email I sent you. I know you get a lot of emails because [NAME OF SHOW] is the place to highlight terrific local businesses like mine. Do you have a minute for me to explain my idea?"

If the person says yes, continue with:

"Great! Would your audience be interested in _____ [AUDIENCE BENEFIT] where we could demonstrate _____ [EXPLAIN VISUAL], because we think it's the perfect time to _____ [HOOK]?"

Fill in the blanks like this:

> Would your audience be interested in learning how to make spooky cupcakes with their kids for Halloween? I own a bakery shop and I'd love to teach your anchors [NAMES OF ANCHORS] to make an awesome spider and crazy eyeball cupcakes. With Halloween just a few weeks away, this would be the perfect time."

Judi Dadtka from It'z My Party Cakery was right on the money!
(Photo courtesy of Fox6Now.com)

After giving your three-sentence "Perfect Pitch," ask your media contact what he or she liked about the idea and if the contact has any suggestions for improving the segment. Listen to what your contact says and adjust accordingly.

If the producer or reporter says, "Yes, that sounds great!" you now have the green light. Ask the producer, "When is the next open segment time you need to fill?" When you get that answer, say "Yes!"

Wow, you must have been super engaging on the phone! Way to go!

Good producers will send you a follow-up email with a guest worksheet to fill out and hopefully, a guest instruction list with details, like where you need to park, when you need to be at the station, and what you need to bring.

In TV, we joke about it being a "communication" business. When something goes wrong and a guest doesn't show up, it's because of poor communication. The joke is more true than funny, so don't let bad communication hurt **YOU**!

When you get booked on a show or by a reporter, it's best for you to follow up by sending a confirmation email, complete with the details of what was agreed upon and pictures or links to other information you discussed. If you have questions prepared for the host, this would be a good time to include them in the email.

What if, after your great phone pitch, the producer or reporter says, "No, I'm not interested in this segment or story right now." Still follow up with an email and include an Outlook contact file attachment with all your information, so your name and number can easily be stored in their contact list.

Thank the person for taking the time to talk and ask that you be kept in mind for any future shows or stories. Then check in with that contact by sending another email every couple of months.

WHAT HAPPENS IF YOU DON'T GET ANYONE ON THE PHONE AT ALL?
Of course, making that first call doesn't always work out quite as easily. You may go right to voicemail, or the producer might say he or she doesn't have time to talk at the moment, or won't even take your call. Now what?

Your best bet is to find out the names, numbers, and emails of the hosts. When hosts come up with ideas for a segment or show, they get bonus points.

IT'S ALL IN A NAME
Speaking of names, how good are you with them? Timing is everything and what if you suddenly get the chance to meet a local TV personality face to face? Do you know his or her name? Are you ready for this encounter?

Over the course of my 20-year-plus career, I've been called many names, some of which I don't care to repeat. As a problem-solving consumer reporter who goes after bad companies, they can call me whatever they want, as long as I solve the problem for the viewer.

However, when people need or want something from me, they should take the time to learn my name. Calling me or writing to me as Katrina Crazy or Bettina Gravy, or "Hey, News Lady," doesn't make me immediately want to invest my time.

> ATT: KRISTIN McCRAVY
> FOX 6 NEWS
> 9001 N. GREEN BAY RD.
> MILWAUKEE WI 53209

Of course, you're a professional and you don't want to make a bad impression. This picture is a fun example to show why you need to be careful.

One of my great friends is a senior producer named Sara Smith. She tells people all the time, "It's Sara without an H, just S-A-R-A." People still wonder why their emails won't go through.

"A Woman's Journey" organizer, Ami Ahuja, was smart. Remember, she was the one who asked me to speak to her group of women entrepreneurs? Ami knew I'd be emceeing the Better Business Bureau Torch Awards and she reached out beforehand.

Her husband, Sonny Ahuja, emailed me to let me know he was on the BBB Board of Directors and he and his wife looked forward to meeting me at the luncheon. Not only did this nice gesture make me feel comfortable and welcome before the event, but now I was waiting for them to introduce themselves.

If you know you're going to meet someone in the media who could be influential, reach out beforehand or a least follow up with an email saying how much you enjoyed what they had to say at the event.

Participants at "A Woman's Journey"
with organizer Ami Ahuja (in red blazer) and her husband, Sonny Ahuja.

But what if you have a chance encounter with someone you know works for a local station, except you can't come up with his or her full name and you don't have time to check your smart phone? Do your best to come up with at least a first name, or don't try using the name at all. Give the person a warm smile, say, "Hi. I just want to tell you how much I enjoy and appreciate your work."

Compliments always pave the way, especially for people on TV. Let them know you have an idea for their show, but you respect their time, and would love to have their business card to email them later. Remember, if this is a chance meeting in a supermarket or the mall, they are probably with their family. A business card is a quick way to get their information.

If they ask, "What's your idea?" Then, of course, give them your pitch, but otherwise don't interrupt their private time. If they're working and you run into them at City Hall while they are waiting for a meeting to start, you might be able to squeeze in a little time.

Again, pave the path with a compliment, and then go with your 30-second elevator speech and what you H.A.V.E. for their show. Or a quick, "Hey, if you're ever in need of an expert on _____ (insert subject here), I'd be glad to help."

Think back to the perfect pitch conversation example above. Still, make it quick. Hand them your card. Ask for their card. Tell them you'll follow up with an email.

Chapter 6
HEY, THIS IS A LIVE REPORT FROM YOUR BUSINESS!

You have officially landed the bigger fish! Oh, sure, you've been interviewed by a reporter for a story before, or maybe you've even done a live in-studio demonstration or interview, but now the live truck is rolling up to YOUR business! This is HUGE!

Instead of the normal 3- to 4-minute segment inside the studio, the morning reporter for the news program or talk show generally has to fill at least 13 to 15 minutes of content over the course of the morning. Each "live" segment usually runs 2 to 3 minutes. The station will need several ideas.

How are you going to help the reporters accomplish their goals and make potential customers remember your business?

You MUST build the relationship with the reporter and ask what he or she wants out of this venture. Like anything else in life, knowing the person's expectations gives you the target for success.

Be sure to convey what you want too. For instance, if you have an awesome machine on the second floor, or a roof-top dining experience, ask the reporter if the photojournalist can shoot from there.

Contrary to what you've seen in the movies, usually the camera is cabled to the live truck. If you want to take the reporter to the roof of your business, you need to tell the crew. They need to decide the best way to run the cable or determine if they need to bring wireless equipment. Do they have wireless equipment? All these questions and decisions need to be made in advance. If the reporter doesn't ask, then you, the business owner, should.

And while having the reporter and the photojournalist come over and discuss everything before you're on "live" would be ideal, rarely do crews make "site visits." They just don't have the time because they're at live locations every day.

Site checks are reserved for locations that might be questionable. Having a crew come and make sure the station engineers can receive a "live" signal from your location isn't always a good thing.

Generally, the conversation to book you on the show and go over some potential segment ideas happens on the phone. Since you won't meet the reporter and photojournalist until about an hour before the first live shot, you need to have your planning discussion at least a week before.

I guarantee you the reporter's boss, the News Director, is looking for segments with "high energy" and "memorable moments." Those have been the buzzwords and the goals since I've been in the business.

You should have fun and play with the audience.

Recently, the morning talk show reporter went to a company called Speedtech International, which makes custom "hook and loop" (Velcro-like) fasteners. Before you start yawning, the place and the employees were TERRIFIC!!

We always love manufacturing because the machines have moving parts and loud sounds. This production facility was even better because the bosses came up with a great tease to keep people watching.

They promised at the end of the show to throw the reporter against a hook-and-loop wall to see if he would stick. They had basically made a Speedwrap T-shirt for him with a special strip that attached between his legs.

Who wouldn't want to watch?! We needed to see if this Speedwrap Onesie was strong enough. Even if the reporter jumped and failed, the attempt would make great TV. Remember, the media needs memorable moments!

Every time the earlier segments were wrapping up, the company representative would tease the reporter and the audience about launching him at the wall.

Their efforts paid off because the audience was paying attention. By the end of the show, we learned how hook-and-loop fasteners are made, how their customers use them in cool ways; and last but not least, we got the money shot at the end.

The reporter bounced onto the wall, stuck at first, but then his weight was too much for the sticky vest with an under-strap.

The moment was hilarious and a little painful judging from the high-pitched squeal coming from Real Milwaukee reporter Chip Brewster.

Memorable moments are the goal of "live" TV.
(Photo courtesy of Fox6Now.com)

My point is: think about how you can play and produce each segment with good moments, leading to a GREAT moment.

You H.A.V.E what it takes! Except now when the TV crew is live at your business or organization, with several segments to fill, you need to expand your Vs. The crew needs to have a lot of VISUALS.

The reporter and photojournalist need to have several different locations, plus different items to pick up, show, and demonstrate.

The News Director won't be happy if the crew keeps showing the same area of your factory. To battle our short attention spans, we need to keep the viewers interested by showing different backdrops. Check out the overall look of a news show. The producers are constantly having the TV hosts sit or stand in different areas of the set.

Walk around your business and start looking for the best areas to show off. You can even put your fingers together like a Hollywood director to capture the best spots.

Going into camera mode works, plus there is the added benefit of people getting curious about what you are doing.

If they ask, take the opportunity to draw your employees into the fun. The more people the better. Like the changing backdrops, we need new voices and different perspectives to chime in.

If you have a diverse work force, flaunt it!

Again, viewers like people who look like them, so give them choices. Your employees might like basking in the limelight too.

I say *limelight* because unlike a spotlight, the limelight highlights everyone on the stage. I'm a strong believer in passing on the praise, and viewers will pick up on the positive vibe of the company.

Even though the reporter will probably only have time to talk with you and a couple of other people, having a crowd of people working in the background is best.

Creating the "busy" look reminds me of a story I heard about Harry Quadracci in the beginning stages of his mega-printing company QuadGraphics.

In his company's early years, when a new, potential client came to see the facility, Quadracci made sure all hands were on deck. Even if the company didn't have a printing job going out that day, employees would drive front loaders around with big rolls of newsprint to make the warehouse look like a bustling place. People are attracted to a party, and customers were drawn into the action.

Besides having employees on deck, sometimes you have to bring in customers. Cool restaurants and bars don't have a lot of people in them at 9 a.m., but I'm sure you have enough loyal friends and family to fill the space between your thumbs. Get the bodies in there and look at how you can make the place sparkle.

Think of your company's TV appearance as if you were staging a house. Clear out anything distracting and stage the rooms to look their best. What seems like a harmless funny sign in the breakroom should go, unless you're planning to talk about it. You don't want the audience trying to read what the sign says behind you instead of listening to you.

Lighting is everything too. Without using a flash, take pictures of the areas you want to highlight. You'll see where you have good natural light and where you'll need to work with the photojournalist on adding more illumination.

Ultimately, the photojournalist will decide where to shoot the segments, but if you do this simple exercise first, you'll know where to lead them quickly.

Be creative and work with the reporter and photojournalist. Chances are they've been doing their jobs for a while and know what works best. Let them decide. Help each other and you'll both make great TV.

Notes

Chapter 7
YOU SURVIVED TV!
GUESS WHAT HAPPENS NOW?!

P op the champagne and have a glass on me. But don't stay out all night. You must prepare for the onslaught of customers. I'm not kidding.

The owner of a Mexican restaurant featured on Fox 6 told one of the station employees that he couldn't believe the response. This restaurant wasn't a new restaurant or having a grand re-opening; our reporter had simply done a quick feature story on its fish fry recipe, which was unique but not new. Because of the story, my friend had an hour and a half wait to get a table and the bar was packed.

TIP 1 - BE READY TO HANDLE INCREASED SALES

We hear these success stories all the time, especially if people really need what the company is selling.

Take for example Theresa Gazdik, who owns a company called Voluptuous Secrets, which sells larger bras. Theresa came to one of my "How to Get Your

Business on TV" classes for the Wisconsin Women's Business Initiative Corporation (WWBIC).

She told me that night she was going to use my "Insider Secrets" to get on TV, and she did! Later that year, she came on Studio A and nailed it. She even had a customer come on the show with her.

Voluptuous Secrets owner Theresa Gazdik nails it and had a customer come on the show with her.
(Photo courtesy of Fox6Now.com)

Later, Theresa and I both received an award from the Wisconsin Women's Business Initiative Corporation, and I asked her what business was like after the segment. Here's what she had to say:

> "It was phenomenal. All these people were coming into my store and I was like, 'Oh, my God! Who is going to take care of all these people?'"

The takeaway: *YOU NEED TO HAVE EXTRA STAFF AVAILABLE JUST IN CASE!*

Theresa said she only had one assistant and the wait to get a proper fitting and bra sometimes took hours. Customers asked how long her store had been there? When she said 12 years, they said they had never heard of her. With a frown, she told me she needed to get a marketing budget and a plan in place. Hopefully, since she's seen the power of television, she'll consider buying commercial time too.

Besides being able to handle the onslaught of sales, you also have to come up with a plan to ride the momentum of landing your first TV segment.

The TV station will most likely post your segment to its website. You are welcome to embed the station's segment link on your own website because more views mean more traffic to the station's site.

Ask them how to obtain the licensing rights and how you can legally use the segment on your website and social media channels without violating copyright laws.

TIP 2 - SHARE THE SEGMENT

Hopefully, you shared with your customers the news of your "Coming Soon" appearance on the show on social media (Facebook, Twitter, Instagram, LinkedIn).

Now, after the show, you should share the show segment link to build your brand with customers you already have, and to attract new ones.

They'll be thinking, "Dang, look at this amazing person on local TV." Let the "Magic Box" work for you.

Better yet, have your current customers work for you too. Offer them a discount, a free drink, a little something, if they share your post with their social media audience.

If you have an email list, send your contacts an email blast with the station's segment link and offer them a deal as well.

You may hate the first time you see and hear yourself on TV, but send the link out anyway. You will be your harshest critic, but you MUST watch. Going over your performance, especially with a coach like me, will only help you get better.

And who knows? You could be a natural!

WHERE TO SHARE YOUR VIDEO

Okay, let's think of all the places you could share the video and get some additional play from your TV segment.

Are you connected to an association or organization that would love to share the good news of your "Magic Box" appearance?

Would your college or university (or even high school) be interested in highlighting an awesome alum?

Would your business friends in a Meetup or Mastermind group want the information to share on their sites or social media accounts? Be sure to offer them a little deal as a thank you for sharing.

How about writing a blog post a week after your appearance about the experience of doing TV? A good title would be, "Wow, I'm Finally Breathing Again."

Steal this text too. "A week has flown by since our company was featured on the news, and I'm finally processing all the emotions bubbling up from such a crazy day."

Tell your readers about your fears and how you overcame them. What hoops did you jump through to be "booked"? What encouraging or interesting comment did the reporter/host say? What part of the TV production process was most surprising?

Last but not least: How has this broadcast BLAST helped your business?

And as an **EXTRA BONUS** for reading this far and "Broadcasting Your Business," send me a copy of your "Wow, I'm Finally Breathing Again" blog post and I'll give you a free critique of the segment, as well as some ideas on how to be booked again.

Enjoy riding this wave—and start thinking about your next pitch.

Tip 3 – How to Pull Another Rabbit Out of the "Magic Box"

First, have you pitched your segment or expert credentials to all the TV stations in your area?

Don't they all deserve a crack at your glowing smile and ways to improve the lives of their viewers? Yes, yes, they do—but beware about how you approach journalists.

I'm about to crack the code you need to pass Media Psychology 101.

Media folks don't actually want to know you've been on another station. Crazy, right?

Seems like a previous performance would be a rubber stamp saying, "Hey, I'm worthy. I didn't melt under pressure. I can do TV." But telling a station you were just on a competing station is the KISS OF DEATH.

You Survived TV! Guess What Happens Now!

You're used. You are old news. We live in the world of "here and now, and we brought this information to you first." If you've been on another station—*GREAT!* —but keep your news bulletin to yourself.

Sure, when we go to your website, we might see the segment you did with the competition. We'll look at the date to be sure you weren't on the other station within the last couple of weeks. Then we'll watch your performance. If you're engaging and you're not pitching us the exact same segment, there's a good chance we'll book you too.

Now, how do you pull another rabbit out of the same station you were on before? You need to come up with another "Hook."

Is there a holiday, social event or news happening you can turn into another pitch? Go back to the H.A.V.E. chapter and start thinking creatively.

Looking back at the guests of 2015, I posted this great example on my LinkedIn page:

And the winner is . . .? Two Men and a Truck for creativity!! Yeah, sorry no actual prize—just GREAT publicity. :) Be creative like Pam Carter, when she pitched the idea of Halloween costumes you can make with a box. Brilliant! It's fun, comes with "viewer benefit" and a cute kid. Now we're talking! Thankfully FOX 6 has the opportunity to highlight terrific local companies. Pam's idea stuck out to me thinking about the guests of 2015. Maybe you'll be on in 2016?

Would you ever think about a moving company doing a Halloween pitch? During Pam's demonstration, she used boxes with the "Two Men and a Truck" logo on them. The company's branding was right out in front. The idea was great for us and the audience, but it was also terrific publicity for the moving company.

To make the segment even better for them, I remember the live shot coming up next wasn't ready yet. Through my ear piece, the producer told me to stretch until the reporter was ready. Pam and "Two Men and a Truck" got about 5 minutes of air time with the logo blazing.

You can't buy that type of publicity, but you can get the coverage for free if you're creative.

Generally, producers would rather have a reasonable interval between your appearances, unless you're a regular expert like a chef or a doctor.

If you only sell products like the "Amazing Chopper," then being booked again on the same station becomes more difficult. TV is a business where if we've "seen it, done that," we don't like to do the same segment again—at least not for a year or two.

Let's say you have a gift shop or a consignment store with different items. You're probably looking at four to six months between segments, depending on how well you "Hook" us with different holiday or seasonal items. Remember, our audience needs new topics.

However, I have seen our shows give a special shout-out to companies we featured for winning a major award or being put into the swag bag for the Golden Globes and Country Music Awards.

If you thank us for the coverage and tell us why the segment helped move your local product into a bigger spotlight, we are more likely to pat you on the back by giving ourselves a little pat too.

You want to keep the relationship going with us. The best way to stay connected is by sending us a simple email every couple of months, or "like" our Tweets or comment on our Facebook pages. You could:

- Comment on a feature you liked on the show.
- Compliment the host's new haircut or amazing dress.
- Tell us about a special accomplishment or award within your industry.
- Updating us on an interesting customer or job assignment you've had and pictures help.

First, TV people always love compliments. Who doesn't? Now you've put your name in our minds again. Secondly, if you have an awesome picture of your interesting job assignment, like an amazing Pool Table

Cake, or you're in a foreign country and you happen to hold up a sign with our show logo, there's a good chance we will give you a shout-out.

If we've featured you before, and you have a special event with a discount for our viewers, producers might do a quick update.

For example,

> Host: "As we go to break, remember Miss Cupcake Bakery in Shorewood we featured last month? They are having a Cupcake War this Saturday for kids ages six to eight. Great for the family and if you mention Real Milwaukee, you get a free cupcake. We'll be right back."

If you consistently keep in touch, you never know when another guest will cancel an appearance and you'll be the "so and so" when the producer says, "Let's see if 'so and so' can fill the spot fast."

Tip 4 – Let the Rabbits Multiply Nationally (They will anyway ☺)

You have nailed down the local stations; have you thought about your national reach?

If you sell your products online, or in national stores, you'd better pack your bags.

Making the Rounds on Local TV Stations

Dr. Harold Katz does. All to save us from bad breath. His "Hook": "Just in time for Valentine's Day. Do you have a kissable mouth?"

Dr. Katz calls himself "America's Bad Breath Doctor." He talks about what foods can give you bad breath, how you can tell if you have bad breath, and why he invented a product to fight the bad-breath battle differently.

Over the years, I've done the segment twice with him, once on our morning show and once in the afternoon. He's made appearances on local stations nationwide talking about his TheraBreath Oral Rinse, sold at Walgreens, Walmart, and Target, just to name a few.

Dr. Harold Katz, "America's Bad Breath Doctor"
(Photo courtesy of Fox6Now.com)

Don't Feel Like Traveling?

Option 1—Contact the National Media

If you H.A.V.E. what it takes for the local media, you also possess all the tools to sell your segment idea to the national media. However, do you have the tools to sell yourself?

National producers have a higher standard for choosing their guests. Show managers must see a level of professionalism, playfulness, and high energy that only comes with multiple appearances on the air.

One experience on TV isn't going to be enough. You need to practice, practice, practice, on different local shows with different host before trying to run with the big dogs.

Heck, with Periscope, Google Chat, and Facebook Live, you can be "live" with an audience all the time. Every bit of real-time talking and interacting helps prepare you for landing a spot on *GOOD MORNING AMERICA* or *TODAY*.

When I was moving up the media chain from little Parkersburg, West Virginia, to Milwaukee, Wisconsin, I was nervous because a bigger market meant more people would be watching me. Before the big move, I revealed my fear to a meteorologist who had known me since I was a 17-year-old intern. He looked me right in the eye and said, "Don't worry about moving to a bigger market. The camera looks the same."

He was right.

You don't see the millions of people. You only see the host, the production crew, and the camera.

If you feel confident and have the experience, take what you H.A.V.E. to the national level.

Option 2 —*A Local Story Could Go National*

Local *show* segments are not shared with affiliate stations nationwide, but local stories or packages (PKG) can be.

The networks have their local stations share stories through a private Internet news feed. The producer in charge of this news feed is responsible for finding stories that could be good for all stations.

Generally, producers want feature stories where the location of the story isn't as important as the story itself. For instance, my recent investigation of "What's Hiding in your Handbag?"

Where the purses were swabbed didn't matter. The gross lab results are what landed this story, the laboratory owner—and me—on stations throughout the county, and even internationally online.

While I wasn't crazy about appearing in a hairnet on *The Daily Mail*, the publicity for Accelerated Analytical Laboratories was huge.

ON AIR – BROADCAST YOUR BUSINESS

Science class: Katrina Cravy of Fox's Contact 6 in Milwaukee, Wisconsin, headed to Accelerated Analytical laboratories to learn how to swab handbags to test for bacteria

Katrina Cravy of Fox's Contact 6 in Milwaukee, Wisconsin, paired up with David Metzger, who owns Accelerated Analytical laboratories, to test just how full-of-germs the average hand bag is.

David said: "The moist environment of a zipped up bag could potentially harbour a fair number of bacteria".

Katrina Cravy of Fox's Contact 6, paired up with David Metzger, who owns Accelerated Analytical laboratories, to test just how full-of-germs the average hand bag is
© Fox News

These images appeared in Britain's *The Daily Mail*.

If your story has "legs" or could run across state lines with interesting information, then ask the reporter if the package could be put on the national feed. He or she will like getting the extra coverage too.

If you don't think about making this suggestion until later, email the assignment desk with a subject line of "Could you mention [REPORTER'S NAME] story for the national feed?" Then in the email write a brief description about why "the subject" has national appeal.

So-called "Mompreneur" stories are great for the national feed list because often the product is geared toward kids. Feature stories travel well, especially if there are cute babies and puppies.

If there is a hot-button issue, and you're the expert, sometimes the national feed producers will send your entire raw (unedited) interview so the affiliate stations can use the comments they want. In many cases, those national producers will choose the best S.O.T.s (Sound on Tape) and only send those comments.

Remember that thanking the reporter or the assignment desk for the coverage also goes a long way.

Even a quick email to the assignment desk or the reporter the next day makes you stand out. Few people give feedback after the story airs. Unless of course, they're upset. Dang that human nature!

ON AIR — BROADCAST YOUR BUSINESS

Option 3 – Jump on the Band Wagon

See if the national store selling your goods has a media plan in place for the local TV stations.

Are they going to highlight items they sell for a big social event or holiday? Ask what you can do to have your product on their display table.

For example, Meijer is a major retail store chain that sells just about everything. For the launch of *Star Wars The Force Awakens*, Meijer's public relations team partnered with local Mueller Communications to make the biggest display I'd ever seen.

You probably aren't selling a *Star Wars* item, but you get the idea of calling the major chains who sell your item to see how they are planning for big social events.

Now THIS is a display table!
(Photo courtesy of Fox6Now.com)

Or how about talking with the local store carrying your product? We had a reporter do a "Hosting a Thanksgiving" segment at a local food market. Even a small mention of your tasty treat or a quick shot of your special candle on the table, can be used in your social media campaign.

Tips for a terrific Turkey Day from Sendik's.
(Photo courtesy of Fox6Now.com)

Option 4 – Find a Face to Give You Space

Local bloggers, lifestyle or fashion experts, or even the PR people for the local mall, might make occasional TV appearances and they need new and exciting products to show off.

Sometimes giving a blogger or expert your product for free is payment enough. Get in touch with the relevant blogger and ask what would be needed to put your product in the mix.

Maureen Fitzgerald, the woman behind the "Wisconsin Mommy" blog, always has great stuff to share with viewers.
(Photo courtesy of Fox6Now.com)

Chapter 8
YES, *YOU* CAN HOLD A NEWS CONFERENCE

Sure, you might think news conferences are only done for big government announcements, or police at crime scenes, but they can be a great tool for other events as well.

Take, for example, my friends at Pixologie. Mollie and Ann are excellent at restoring old photos and organizing digital files. Remember, I consulted with

Save Your Photos Day, September 27, 2014.

ON AIR — BROADCAST YOUR BUSINESS

them and found their super-fast scanner demonstration perfect for TV.

An event to save photos of the Charles Allis Art Museum and Allis Chalmers Co. that tell the impact they have had in Milwaukee.

The Allis Chalmers Corporation, at one time the largest employer in Wisconsin, was a vital part of Milwaukee for the last century. Charles and Sarah Allis' mansion and world class art collection have been a prominent part of Milwaukee's art scene since the Allis' bequeathed it to us in 1947.

The Charles Allis Art Museum would love to scan your photos of both the museum and corporation that bear the Allis name.

In addition to photos we want to document your unique stories behind them. Given the impact that the Charles Allis Art Museum and Allis Chalmers Corporation have had in Milwaukee for over 100 years, we know there are many photos out there, both vintage and current that tell many stories!

CHARLES ALLIS
ART MUSEUM
1801 N Prospect Ave.
Milwaukee, WI 53202

SEPTEMBER 12, 2015
1:00 PM – 5:00 PM

News release graphic of Allis Chalmers

About a year later, they were hired by the Charles Allis Art Museum to collect and restore old photos of the Allis Chalmers Manufacturing Company, which had been a huge employer in the Milwaukee area for years.

The museum only had a few photos of what the company used to look like inside. Now they needed to ask the public for help to find more.

Mollie asked me what they should do to get coverage and I said," You should hold a news conference."

"Us? We can hold a news conference?" she asked.

"Yes, you can, and bringing all the people together actually makes the job easier for the media," I replied.

The timing was perfect. Labor Day was the Monday before the Museum's big Saturday event. People could come to the museum, bring their old photos of the company and get them scanned for free. In addition, the story was about the history of work done by hundreds of Wisconsinites over the years. The "retirees" were the media "Hook."

Plus, since Labor Day is a holiday, the folks at Pixologie experienced two bonus media facts:

1. Government and business offices are closed, which means the media is more likely to do softer news stories, since we don't have regular "day-of" news to handle.

2. Newsrooms usually have fewer staff because people take the day off.

If you provide what the media calls "One-Stop Shopping," where everyone we need to interview is in one place, then you're more likely to get coverage.

THREE KEY PEOPLE AT A NEWS CONFERENCE
During our informal coaching session, I gave Mollie my first "Media Map." I outlined how Pixologie could attract the media by offering three "key" people at their news conference:

1. The "It's Personal" person/family
2. The Authority Figure
3. The Concerned Person

The **"It's Personal"** person is the MOST important because a reporter must have that individual do a longer and more complete package. Without the number-one person, you'll probably only see a VO/SOT (Voice Over / Sound on Tape) with the authority figure on TV giving only one sound bite. The whole news story would last about 45 seconds or so.

As fate (or luck) would have it, Mollie found a great woman whose parents met at Allis Chalmers. She wouldn't be alive without the company! This woman happened to come into the Pixologie offices a couple weeks before, plus she was willing to talk on camera about it. Thank you, Universe!

Next, the media needs the **Authority Figure** to describe why the event is happening in the first place. The head of the Charles Allis Art Museum was there. And as **concerned photo historians**, Mollie and/or Ann had to explain how the photos were going to be handled.

The "Media Map" I gave Mollie was a slight variation of my *"three and me"* theory. When I was a street reporter, often we had to turn in two stories a day on separate subjects. The workload could be brutal, but I would tell my photojournalist, "All we need to do is get three and me." We were always looking for three interviews. One person who was in favor of the topic, one against it and the authority figure to tell people what was the next step and what the issue should mean to them.

The news conference was a success! Hundreds of photos were scanned and their client, the Charles Allis Museum, was happy.
(Photo courtesy of Fox6Now.com)

For a story with no controversy (a "soft news" feature), Mollie followed my map. She did NOT forget the "Call to Action" (CTA) to inform viewers how they could be part of the story and get their photos scanned for free.

In the end, two out of four stations came to the news conference, and the producer of my afternoon show booked them for a live interview without my even asking or knowing they had been booked. Good for them!

The Saturday scanning event was successful. Hundreds of photos were scanned and the Museum—the Pixologie client—was happy.

Here's a tidbit from the email Mollie sent me after their Labor Day launch:

> "PS—I keep pinching myself that we really held a press conference!!! Bold, very bold! :) Can't thank you enough for the direction—and the angle of the retirees."

Sometimes casting the "Hook" just takes the right spin, the right timing, and the right people. Of course, some good direction doesn't hurt. ☺

My "Media Map"

I like helping clients figure out the right bait and make a good "Media Map." Here's my "Media Map" for a do-it-yourself news conference:

1. Pick a day and time.
2. Pick a place.
3. Send out a mass news release.
4. Set up the venue.
5. Prepare visuals.

Okay, let's go into some detail about each of these points.

1. Pick a Day and Time that Make Sense

Think about the event you're highlighting and how many days it will really take people to prepare after seeing the segment.

For instance, the "Please Bring Your Pictures to The Museum Event" meant it would take a few days for viewers to find the pictures.

If you have a "Let's Dance the Night Away Fundraiser" for Saturday night, then try to get booked the Wednesday, Thursday, or Friday right before the event. People generally make their weekend plans just a few days ahead.

The date also has to work for all the "key people" you need at the news conference, so check their schedules first.

2. Pick a Place with Great Backdrops and Different Visuals

The Charles Allis Museum was a great location because there are different rooms and artwork all around. Let's say you're not as lucky. Look around your place and choose the most visually appealing backdrop. Put your central news conference there.

If you have other places you'd like to show off, by all means, take the media on a tour. Just like any good party, we like to see other rooms in the house.

Take us out to the manufacturing plant, or right into the kitchen to see how the chefs are making delicious meals. You get the picture. We need a lot of different images.

3. Send Out a Mass News Release with the Who, What, When, and Why to All Stations and Media Outlets. Don't Forget Bloggers Interested in Your Topic

This email isn't as personal as the emails you've sent directly to the producer for a particular show. This one has to have mass appeal, although you can still use the lessons in the "Killer Email" template.

Except, before the first sentence of niceties, let the station know this is a "One-Stop Shopping" story. Be sure to highlight the important key people who will all be there at once, and announce that there will be a chance for one-on-one interviews.

Send out this release to all the assignment editors at least a week in advance to make sure you get on the agenda for the morning news meeting. During this meeting, managers and reporters discuss what they're going to cover for the day.

While you're excited about hosting a news conference, unfortunately it's not a party and the stations won't send you an R.S.V.P. to let you know someone is coming. They don't take the time to do so, because honestly, they're not sure they can make any commitments. Breaking news is always a possibility and the crew could be diverted.

If your news conference or event is before 9:00 a.m., send the release early. This will give the station a chance to schedule an early reporter/photojournalist the day before.

4. Set Up the Venue with a Podium. Also Set Up "Break Away" Areas that Have Good Visual Backgrounds for One-on-One Interviews

It's always good to have a podium in case a photojournalist comes without a reporter to hold the microphone. The podium provides them with a flat surface for them to set the mic on. It's not always necessary. Don't feel like you have to go and buy a podium.

While the media may like getting the "nuts and bolts," or the who, what, when, and where at the podium with all the stations rolling, we also like to get our own one-on-one interviews.

For instance, we'd like to interview the woman who owed her life to Allis-Chalmers in a one-on-one setting. We need B-roll footage of her looking over her family albums to reinforce the story before getting to her interview.

If you can provide several little areas for break-away interviews to be done after the news conference, let the stations know that's available. Usually they can figure out how to take turns interviewing people separately and efficiently.

5. Prepare Demonstrations, Videos, Photos, and for an Added Bonus, Share Copies

If you have video or pictures you'd like to share with the media, you have a few options. You can blow up the pictures and have them simply video tape the pictures, or you can give them a USB flash drive with copies of the pictures or video. You can also post all of these to your website gallery and hand them business cards with the link.

A cool little flash drive with your logo, though, might have them thinking about your company for years to come, especially if that little drive has made the rounds for transferring files at the station.

Taking a break with my husband, Scott, during the Wisconsin MS 150 Bike Tour.

My view from emceeing the 2016 MS Walk.

Chapter 9

THE POWER OF FREE STUFF, CELEBRITY STATUS, AND CLEVER IDEAS

I was a Resident Advisor at the University of Southern California during my sophomore, junior, and senior years. I learned a lot about people from all walks of life. Did you know they all have something in common? *They like to eat.*

People love free food. My floor meetings were well attended if Mr. Pizza or Ms. Cookies had also been invited.

Nothing has changed.

If you send the station free anything, you have a better chance of being heard. The best Public Relations (PR) people I know started our relationship off with a gallon of coffee and a few bagels or donuts for the staff, just so they could have 15 minutes of face time. Brilliant!

Why not come in behind the Trojan Horse of hot dogs or subs to get a lunch meeting? After a few bites and a little chit-chat, then ask them how you, or your product, can be of service to the station.

The media is more likely to say yes to a PR firm or company with a big outreach, but if you seem like a nice person, and have something to benefit our audience, then there is a good chance we'll open the door.

Getting to know a producer or reporter face to face is a great advantage for gathering insight into the media world, how they run the show, what stories they are looking for, and what will really help their audience. All questions you should ask.

Let's say when you call asking for a quick meeting, the producer or reporter says, "We don't have time for that." Just before they are about to end the call, say, "No problem. I'll go ahead and send this goodness your way and anything you can do will be great."

They can't help but have a warm feeling for you after eating your goodies and doing nothing in return. Perhaps they will do something for you the next time you call.

Don't Forget the Viewers

You can also offer something free or discounted for the viewers. If the show producer likes your product, you'd be surprised how often this works at getting you free publicity—especially if you're local.

For instance, check out these dry-erase boards from DryMaps. The local company gave a discount code for "FOX6" to get 30 percent off. Not only did we air the video of the company's commercial, we also played a game using these cute Wisconsin DryMaps they sent us.

DryMaps offers a great learning tool and discount for viewers.
(Photo courtesy of Fox6Now.com)

Sending your products straight to the host of the show is also a great idea, especially if you're asking the host to post a picture with the product to create some social media buzz. Hosts usually have a pretty big following and they are always looking for creative and funny pictures to post.

Want two great examples? Sure you do.

1. Shine Bright with Holiday Lights

This is one of the best press kits I've received lately for the Holiday Lights Celebration put on by Milwaukee Downtown. Local Ellingsen Brady Advertising made this happen.

Angelica Duria tweets about the Twitter campaign—
Take an "Elfie" for Milwaukee's Holiday Lights Festival #elfie2015.

The press kit was personalized and came with an elf hat, peppermint sticks, and an elf ornament with my picture. They did this for all the on-air personalities. Wow! All the promotional items came with the same request: Please take an "Elfie" and share the picture on social media to let people know about Milwaukee's Holiday Lights Festival.

Judging from the pictures and Milwaukee Downtown's Annual Report, this campaign was a success.

> **Milwaukee Downtown's Annual Report**
> - Kick-Off Extravaganza – Organized the city's largest switch-flipping ceremony in Pere Marquette Park with 2,200 guests. Families were treated to live music, dancing, ice carving, a visit from Santa, a 10-minute fireworks show and free Jingle Bus rides, of which 464 passengers took advantage.
> - Social Media – Utilizing Facebook, Twitter and Instagram, the festival was able to reach 941,735 social media users and generate 2,184,714 impressions. Total engagement was 64,841 and follower growth increased by 52% since 2013.

Of course, not everyone has a marketing budget. Luckily, you have options.

2. Love Your Melon Beanies

Without spending a dime, email the host first to see if he or she is interested in your idea or product before you send it.

Check out this perfect "gauging your interest" email example:

> **Subject: Love Your Melon**
> Hi Katrina!
> My name's Trina Do, and I'm a part of this organization called Love Your Melon at UW Oshkosh. The mission of LYM is to put a cozy and warm hat on EVERY child fighting cancer in America! In the last day or so alone, we've raised over $300,000 for childhood cancer support and research. Our website is www.loveyourmelon.com for more info!
>
> We need YOUR help with something, Katrina! We'd love to have your support in our mission to change the lives of children battling cancer. We'd love to send you a free LYM beanie in trade for a selfie or a mention on Fox6! If you could give us a shout out/ post about us wearing your beanie and tag @LoveYourMelon, it would be so wonderful!
>
> Thank you for your consideration! We'd love if you could help us out and show your support for these amazing and strong children battling cancer. I really hope to hear back from you soon!
>
> Kindly,
> Trina Do
> =======
> Trina Do, Junior I Student Nurse
> University of Wisconsin Oshkosh
> College of Nursing
> UWO Love Your Melon Crew Captain

First, this University of Wisconsin–Oshkosh student was an upbeat, quick, and clear writer. I could see and hear her smile through her words.

Who wouldn't want to help kids fighting cancer?

Who wouldn't want to help out a college student who is asking nicely?

Who wouldn't want this awesome beanie?

Someone from a different college campus sent a similar email to my General Manager. Done!

This email campaign must have sealed the deal all over the nation because, when I went to buy a few for my family, they were sold out.

What do both these campaigns have in common?

They are tapping into the large social media following of people on traditional media. To pull off this maneuver correctly, you must have a product with viewer benefit like a great community event or a beanie that gives back.

It doesn't hurt to have a fun hashtag like #elfie2015 or #loveyourmelon to track how much play you received.

Celebrity Status

Like it or not, our society is often driven by celebrity status. Having your product endorsed or even *"liked"* by a celebrity can help.

Major corporations pay major celebrities major money to endorse what they're selling. But what if you're not major yet?

If you're a non-profit with a big event coming up, have you considered inviting a local TV or radio personality to emcee the event? Stations want to promote their product (the on-air folks) for doing good things in the community, and are more likely to cover your event if one of their personalities are emceeing.

Most stations' websites have a Community Affairs section where you can submit your request. You can also email the on-air person first and ask if he or she would be interested in emceeing. Hosts' email addresses are usually on their bio page or in the "About" section of their Facebook pages.

If they say," Yes, I'd love to be part of your event!" Great!

Most likely, you'll still have to fill out the form and get the event cleared by the station's management. This step is basically a rubber stamp, although once my station declined a request for me.

The Ozaukee County Republicans had heard me talking on the radio about my college days when I interned for former President Ronald Reagan after his term in office. The group wanted me to come and share the same memories I told on-air, but the station wasn't comfortable with having me at a political organization for fear of looking biased.

Just so you know, most television personalities do these extra events for FREE simply because it's good community relations. Similarly, the majority of news departments don't allow their "talent" to be paid because of the possible appearance of a conflict of interest.

Let's say the law firm of Dewey, Cheatum, and Howe pays me to be its keynote speaker at an event, and later I learn the accountant of the law firm had been embezzling money. The station would be concerned about the fairness of my reporting the embezzlement story since the accountant had cut me a check.

Radio personalities typically don't have this concern or requirement. They are usually paid by the company or organization asking them to come to the event. It's always best to ask the station how it handles payment for speaking engagements.

Okay, you've secured the local celebrity—which means you automatically secured local coverage, right? Not so fast!

The local celebrity/your emcee won't be thinking about your agenda. To most of them, the event is just another part of their duties to be handled when the time comes. They will not be alerting the assignment desk and making sure a photojournalist can come and get video of them speaking. Sometimes the Community Affairs people will contact the assignment editor, but don't take chances with your coverage.

You still need to send the news release to the station with the Who, What, and When, plus be sure to put the name of their on-air talent/your emcee in the subject line.

To make a bigger media splash, provide the on-air talent/your emcee some social media copy with all the Twitter handles and Facebook event links they'll need to promote the event.

Tell your celebrities how much you would appreciate their copying-and-pasting the text to post on their social media accounts because you are sure people would LOVE to see them in person. Flattery, oh, flattery—you are our kryptonite!

Remember that even though the TV personality isn't paid to do your event, please make sure you've handled paying for parking, their meal, and any incidentals to make your event a pleasure to attend. This appreciation and attention to detail will help your organization stand out the next time you ask.

A thank-you note also goes a long way. You'd be surprised how few people actually send a follow-up thank-you note. If you put a small gift card to Starbucks or a local restaurant in there, you're golden.

TV and radio personalities aren't the only local celebrities either. Think about the people who get media attention: the well-known names in your community like local athletes, college coaches, heads of major companies, school district superintendents, etc. If the media likes interviewing such people, and they have a big social media following, see if they'd be willing to get involved.

CONTESTS AND OTHER CLEVER IDEAS

You've likely heard the phrase, "Cream rises to the top?" "Clever" has a way of putting you above the rest.

A contest is a clever way to get the media pop. This can bubble over to social media as well.

Check out this email:

> To: Cravy, Katrina
> Subject: New campaign humorously warns homeowners on dangers of DIY
>
> Hi Katrina,
> I hope you're well! I wanted to send a quick note and let you know of a recent campaign that's sure to catch the interest of your FOX 6 audience.

Free Stuff, Local Celebrity Status & Clever Ideas

—75 percent of homeowners have completed a DIY project in the past three years.

—40 percent, unfortunately, wished they hadn't.

Examples of these everyday real-life 'DIY fail' stories, from a tree falling on a house to a bathroom flooded in toilet tank water, are serving as the inspiration behind Allstate's latest "Mayhem DIY" campaign. Using the brand's familiar Mayhem character, these stories come to life in TV spots that demonstrate the dangers of conducting DIY projects without being fully prepared or properly covered. Teasers from the commercials will air next week.

This is where your audience comes in—from Thursday, Dec. 31 until Wednesday, Jan. 6, the general public will have the opportunity to vote online and on Twitter for their favorite DIY fail ad to run in its entirety. Through their participation, they will automatically be entered into an hourly sweepstakes for a chance to win a variety of DIY tools, with **one grand prize winner receiving a $25,000 gift card to Lowe's!**

What makes this a good pitch?

Number one, the **bold letters** throughout the email help you **track the key points**. Number two, the media gets a little nugget of "new" news from a survey with the stats mentioned in the email.

A good DIY gone-wrong story is usually pretty funny— unless, of course, someone loses an eye. Then it's not.

THE MEDIA LOVES SURVEYS AND STUDIES

The results give us a way to categorize people. Viewers learn where they fit into society, and hosts can chime in about their lives and experiences.

This pitch is also good because there is a "Call To Action" for viewers to get involved in a contest and win something big! Super!

Keep thinking about how the host has to tease the story with a magazine-style headline. "Coming up today

Allstate Insurance Company's Mayhem commercial.

Dove Real Beauty Sketches commercial

on Studio A—Need to do some home improvements? See how you can win a $25,000 gift card to Lowe's!"

We get the viewers. You get the publicity.

Not to mention, **the station will probably play your commercial during the actual broadcast.** We did for this segment!

The media will also talk about CLEVER commercials. Dove wins the award here for its campaign to help women realize they are all beautiful.

Remember, the media's key demographic is women. If you're selling a women's empowerment message, then expect the media to jump on and carry the flag.

And don't forget our attachment to our children. The Pandora ad on the next page made us get weepy.

Pandora's Unique Connection commercial.

We had to show the entire commercial of blindfolded children recognizing their mothers' faces simply by touch. We then talked about our feelings and our own experiences as children or moms.

The moral of the story here: A cool social experiment video will increase your chances for talk show hosts to talk about your findings and your company.

IT ALL COMES DOWN TO THIS: CONTENT!

Content is what drives the media. By this I mean good visual information that is timely and enriches our lives.

Of course, your product, your company, your organization, was created to do good and provide people with a better experience. I know that's why I started my company and wrote this book.

I want to help you craft your story and broadcast your business, whether you're a small business owner, a non-profit group, or a public relations firm who wants the best for its clients.

Give the media something to truly offer viewers, and you'll be offered a spot on TV and the attention you deserve.

Remember the world is waiting to fall in love with your story. You just have to know how to tell it!

Final Thoughts

Wow! If you read that all in one sitting, I'm sure your head is spinning and your butt is sore. Get up and move around. You're amazing!

If you read this book piece by piece, hopefully you're starting to digest each bite. The good news is now you have a resource to continually go over and see if your pitch and presentation are meeting the mark.

Making the first call or sending that first email doesn't have to be absolutely perfect. What's the saying? "The need to be perfect often keeps people doing perfectly nothing." Don't be that person. Trust yourself enough to know you'll make mistakes and they will turn into lessons.

Truthfully, fun mistakes on TV are what people will remember. Moments when the host or the guest are laughing about what just happened will have the audience laughing and retaining the information too. Have FUN!

The audience WILL fall in love with your story. They WON'T if they don't get to hear it.

You, your product, and your company or organization, deserve the attention of the media. After more than 20 years in the business, I know how we think. This book was designed to be a map inside the media's brain. Your mission is to follow the path and find the beautiful "Promised Land" of publicity.

Thank you for taking your first step with me.

DON'T GIVE UP!

As with any journey, the roads aren't always smooth and the air conditioning doesn't always work. If you need some help, please give me a call or go to my website (www.katrinacravy.com) for more information. We can set up some one-on-one coaching and I can also do a half-day or whole day training session for the entire staff.

Let's get together and broadcast your business.

GOT SOME FEEDBACK?
I'D LOVE TO HEAR FROM YOU!

I hope you enjoyed what you learned in *ON AIR: Insider Secrets to Attract the Media and Get Free Publicity.* During the early morning hours when I was writing this book, I was surprised by what flowed out of my noodle.

When you've been doing something for so long, you take for granted how much you've learned over the years.

Final Thoughts

I'm grateful my broadcast brain switched on, and I know there are some hidden pieces of knowledge yet to find.

Of course, like anything, this book is still a work in progress. If you think I forgot something, you're confused by a section, or you simply want to talk more, please let me know. I'd love to get your feedback.

Email me at Katrina.Cravy@KatrinaCravy.com or leave a comment on my social media pages.

Let's spread the love. It's time to **BROADCAST YOUR BUSINESS!**

Acknowledgments

For we walk by faith, not by sight.
—2 Corinthians 5:7

God put the desire to start this book and this business in my heart, even though I kept telling Him, "Hey, You're asking me to jump off a cliff!" I can't tell where this adventure will eventually take my family, and somehow, I keep feeling it's going to be okay. I hope you can feel, question, and know His love too.

Now to the "earthly" thank yous:

To make this list shorter, I'm going to acknowledge everyone I know—because you've all influenced me in some way. Okay, done!

Not good enough? All right, here's the best short version I can do.

Thanks to my brother, Robby—or Rob, now (such a big boy), who has always been a good sounding board, and to my grandmother, Lilian, who knows how to tell a good story.

Have you heard the one about a woman who loves her mother-in-law? Because I do. Jane Powell is one of my best friends; my life wouldn't be the same without her.

Plus Jane gave birth to my husband, Scott Powell, who has always supported me and didn't squash this crazy business idea.

Scott also put me in touch with designer Rachael Bertsch, who came up with my logo and branding, and then called her friend, photographer Brian Slawson, who made me look better than real life.

I also appreciate Alyssa Otter and Ian Baxter at Swarming Technologies, who created my first website and told me I shouldn't name the company "Katapult" because my own name is what people know. Great advice, great work. Thanks also to EPIC Creative for super-charging my message.

Then I would like to thank "my girls." They were my Board of Directors when I didn't even have a company yet. I'm listing you in the order I met you, not to be confused with the level of importance (unless you want to take it that way): Kendall Miller, Aime Rowe, Kimberly Buchanan, Susan Kim, Vivian King, Anne Brown, Molly Fay, Susanne Barthel, Jennifer Lehman, Pam Stater, Sara Smith, Cassandra McShepard, Nicole Koglin, Nikki Packee, and Aleta Norris.

ACKNOWLEDGMENTS

Also, many thanks to our life-long family friends, Aunt Daryl and Uncle Wes Lusher, who—besides being terrific people, also happen to be great proofreaders. I couldn't have finished this project without their critical eyeballs, along with those of Kendall Miller and my mother, Kathy Chandler. A special thanks to my mom for lending her legal services and devoted attention to this project. No one loves you like your mother.

A great deal of gratitude goes to FOX 6 General Manager Chuck Steinmetz, who believed in me and gave me so many wonderful opportunities at the station. Plus, I'd be remiss not to thank the man who first hired me at WITI, News Director Bob Clinkingbeard, and the boss who didn't fire me, News Director John LaPorte. ☺ I have learned so much from these two!

And, of course, my Clovis High School journalism teacher, David Menendian, who still keeps in touch. I think I'll send him a copy of this book!

About the Author & Broadcast Your Business

Katrina Cravy is a former Emmy award-winning Consumer Reporter and TV host who wore headgear to high school. Her fun-loving and "get-the-job-done" style has made her one of the most trusted and well-known names in southeastern Wisconsin.

With more than 20 years of media experience, she is now sharing her insider secrets about what companies must H.A.V.E. to attract the media and thousands of new customers.

She's also enjoying her husband, son, their two cats, and any time she gets to play tennis and visit her family in California.

You can contact Katrina through Facebook, Twitter, and though her website, www.KatrinaCravy.com. She would love to hear from you!